GED® Test 5-Hour Quick Prep

for dummies®
A Wiley Brand

GED® Test 5-Hour Quick Prep

by Tim Collins, PhD

GED® Test 5-Hour Quick Prep For Dummies®

Published by: **John Wiley & Sons, Inc.,** 111 River Street, Hoboken, NJ 07030-5774, www.wiley.com

Copyright © 2024 by John Wiley & Sons, Inc., Hoboken, New Jersey

Published simultaneously in Canada

No part of this publication may be reproduced, stored in a retrieval system or transmitted in any form or by any means, electronic, mechanical, photocopying, recording, scanning or otherwise, except as permitted under Sections 107 or 108 of the 1976 United States Copyright Act, without the prior written permission of the Publisher. Requests to the Publisher for permission should be addressed to the Permissions Department, John Wiley & Sons, Inc., 111 River Street, Hoboken, NJ 07030, (201) 748-6011, fax (201) 748-6008, or online at http://www.wiley.com/go/permissions.

Trademarks: Wiley, For Dummies, the Dummies Man logo, Dummies.com, Making Everything Easier, and related trade dress are trademarks or registered trademarks of John Wiley & Sons, Inc. and may not be used without written permission. GED and GED Testing Services are registered trademarks of American Council on Education ("ACE"). All other trademarks are the property of their respective owners. John Wiley & Sons, Inc. is not associated with any product or vendor mentioned in this book.

LIMIT OF LIABILITY/DISCLAIMER OF WARRANTY: WHILE THE PUBLISHER AND AUTHORS HAVE USED THEIR BEST EFFORTS IN PREPARING THIS WORK, THEY MAKE NO REPRESENTATIONS OR WARRANTIES WITH RESPECT TO THE ACCURACY OR COMPLETENESS OF THE CONTENTS OF THIS WORK AND SPECIFICALLY DISCLAIM ALL WARRANTIES, INCLUDING WITHOUT LIMITATION ANY IMPLIED WARRANTIES OF MERCHANTABILITY OR FITNESS FOR A PARTICULAR PURPOSE. NO WARRANTY MAY BE CREATED OR EXTENDED BY SALES REPRESENTATIVES, WRITTEN SALES MATERIALS OR PROMOTIONAL STATEMENTS FOR THIS WORK. THE FACT THAT AN ORGANIZATION, WEBSITE, OR PRODUCT IS REFERRED TO IN THIS WORK AS A CITATION AND/OR POTENTIAL SOURCE OF FURTHER INFORMATION DOES NOT MEAN THAT THE PUBLISHER AND AUTHORS ENDORSE THE INFORMATION OR SERVICES THE ORGANIZATION, WEBSITE, OR PRODUCT MAY PROVIDE OR RECOMMENDATIONS IT MAY MAKE. THIS WORK IS SOLD WITH THE UNDERSTANDING THAT THE PUBLISHER IS NOT ENGAGED IN RENDERING PROFESSIONAL SERVICES. THE ADVICE AND STRATEGIES CONTAINED HEREIN MAY NOT BE SUITABLE FOR YOUR SITUATION. YOU SHOULD CONSULT WITH A SPECIALIST WHERE APPROPRIATE. FURTHER, READERS SHOULD BE AWARE THAT WEBSITES LISTED IN THIS WORK MAY HAVE CHANGED OR DISAPPEARED BETWEEN WHEN THIS WORK WAS WRITTEN AND WHEN IT IS READ. NEITHER THE PUBLISHER NOR AUTHORS SHALL BE LIABLE FOR ANY LOSS OF PROFIT OR ANY OTHER COMMERCIAL DAMAGES, INCLUDING BUT NOT LIMITED TO SPECIAL, INCIDENTAL, CONSEQUENTIAL, OR OTHER DAMAGES.

For general information on our other products and services, please contact our Customer Care Department within the U.S. at 877-762-2974, outside the U.S. at 317-572-3993, or fax 317-572-4002. For technical support, please visit https://hub.wiley.com/community/support/dummies.

Wiley publishes in a variety of print and electronic formats and by print-on-demand. Some material included with standard print versions of this book may not be included in e-books or in print-on-demand. If this book refers to media such as a CD or DVD that is not included in the version you purchased, you may download this material at http://booksupport.wiley.com. For more information about Wiley products, visit www.wiley.com.

Library of Congress Control Number: 2023948371

ISBN 978-1-394-23174-4 (pbk); ISBN 978-1-394-23176-8 (ebk); ISBN 978-1-394-23175-1 (ebk)

SKY10063602_010224

Contents at a Glance

Start Here 1

BLOCK 1: GED Overview in 20 Minutes. 3

BLOCK 2: Preparing for the Test 21

BLOCK 3: Working Through Some Practice Questions 43

BLOCK 4: Taking a (Shortened) Practice Test. 103

BLOCK 5: Ten Tips for the Night Before Your Test 151

Index 155

Table of Contents

START HERE...1
    About This Book..1
    Foolish Assumptions..1
    Icons Used in This Book...2
    Where to Go from Here...2

BLOCK 1: GED Overview in 20 Minutes.........................3
    Registering for the Test..4
        Knowing if you're eligible.................................4
        Choosing when and where to take the test......4
        Asking for accommodations or language options......5
        Signing up for your test.................................6
    Identifying What to Bring to the Test...................6
    Knowing What to Expect During the Test............7
        Understanding exam room rules.................7
        Identifying computer skills you need............7
        The order, topics, and time for each test......9
        Navigating the question types................13
    Discovering Important Test-Taking Strategies......15
        Managing stress.......................................16
        Watching the clock: Using your time wisely......16
        Addressing and answering questions............17
        Guess for success: Using intelligent guessing......17
        Leaving time for review.............................18
    Understanding Your Score...................................19
        Identifying how scores are determined........19
        Retaking a test to improve your score........19

BLOCK 2: Preparing for the Test...............................21
    Exploring the Language Arts Test.......................21
        Choosing wisely in the reading component......21
        Succeeding on the extended response essay......23
        Tackling grammar and language questions......27
    Surveying the Social Studies Test.......................29
        Questions about text passages.................29
        Questions about visual materials..............30
    Peering into the Science Test.............................33
        Understanding the test format and topics......34
        Analyzing scientific text passages............35
        Interpreting graphs, tables, and other visual materials......36
    Sizing Up the Math Test...................................39
        Identifying the math skills you need............39
        Using a calculator, formula sheets, and special symbols......40

BLOCK 3: Working Through Some Practice Questions......43
    Reasoning through Language Arts Sample Questions......43
        RLA Reading Comprehension.................43
        A Sample Extended Response Prompt......49
        RLA Grammar and Language....................51

Social Studies Sample Questions 58
    Questions 58
    Answers and explanations 69
Science Sample Questions 73
    Questions 73
    Answers and explanations 88
Mathematical Reasoning Sample Questions 91
    Questions 91
    Answers and explanations 97

BLOCK 4: **Taking a (Shortened) Practice Test** 103
Reasoning through Language Arts Practice Test 103
    Reading comprehension and grammar and usage 104
    Extended Response 112
Social Studies Practice Test 116
Science Practice Test 125
Math Practice Test 131
Answers and Explanations 138
    Reasoning through Language Arts answers .138
    Extended Response sample 141
    Social Studies answers 142
    Science answers 144
    Math answers 146

BLOCK 5: **Ten Tips for the Night Before Your Test** 151
Know Your Time-Management Strategies 151
Review Strategies for Analyzing and Answering Questions 152
Take a Practice Test 152
Practice Your Stress-Coping Strategies 152
Set Up Your Test Area or Plan Your Route to the Test Site 152
Lay Out Comfortable Clothes 153
Have Your Picture ID Ready 153
Work with the Computer, Calculator, and Formula Sheet 153
Visualize Success! 154
Getting Good Rest the Week Before the Test 154

INDEX 155

Start Here

Maybe you're struggling in your career, you want to apply to college, or you want to set a good example for your kids. Whatever your reasons for taking the GED, the test can help you get ahead if you don't have a high school diploma. This book helps you to prepare for the computer-based GED test, which, if you pass, offers you the equivalent of a high-school diploma without attending all the classes.

About This Book

GED Test 5-Hour Quick Prep For Dummies helps you earn a high-school diploma in the shortest time possible. If you can prepare yourself for a series of challenging test sections that determine whether you've mastered key skills, you can get a GED diploma that's the equivalent of a high-school education — and you can do so in much less than four years.

This friendly instruction manual helps you succeed on the all-computerized GED test. Use this book as your first stop. It isn't a subject-matter preparation book — that is, it doesn't take you through the basics of math and then progress into algebra, geometry, and so on. It does, however, prepare you for the GED test by organizing your time into study blocks that add up to five hours:

>> **Block 1 (20 minutes):** Get an overview of the GED, including how to sign up, what to expect, and how to understand your score.

>> **Block 2 (30 minutes):** This block explains what you need to know for each part of the GED and offers tips for preparing and successfully answering the questions.

>> **Block 3 (1 hour):** The sample questions help you understand the questions you'll be asked and how the GED might ask them. You can use this block to practice only the questions you recognize and/or use the explanations to understand the questions and answers you need to review.

>> **Block 4 (3 hours, 5 minutes):** The shortened practice test with detailed explanations helps you practice not only answering questions, but also taking the timed test. Although this isn't a full-length practice test, the shortened version will still help you check your understanding of the material, as well as answer all those questions in test-like conditions, while still keeping your preparation time to five hours.

>> **Block 5 (5 minutes):** This short block gives you ten things to check, review, or prepare the night before the test, like planning your route and laying out comfy clothes.

Foolish Assumptions

When I wrote this book, I made a few assumptions about you, dear reader. Here's who I think you are:

>> You're serious about earning your GED as quickly as you can.

>> You've made earning a GED a priority in your life because you want to advance in the workplace or move on to college.

>> You're willing to give up some activities so that you have the time to prepare, always keeping in mind your other responsibilities, too.

>> You meet your state's requirements regarding age, residency, and the length of time since leaving school that make you eligible to take the GED test. (You can find these on the GED Testing Service's website, https://ged.com.)

>> You have sufficient English language skills to handle the test (or sufficient Spanish language skills if you take the test in Spanish).

>> You want a fun and friendly guide that helps you achieve your goal.

If any of these descriptions sounds like you, welcome aboard. I've prepared an enjoyable tour of the GED test.

Icons Used in This Book

Icons — little pictures you see in the margins of this book — highlight bits of text that you want to pay special attention to. Here's what each one means:

TIP

Whenever we want to tell you a special trick or technique that can help you succeed on the GED test, we mark it with this icon. Keep an eye out for this guy.

REMEMBER

This icon points out information you want to burn into your brain. Think of the text with this icon as the sort of stuff you'd tear out and put on a bulletin board or your refrigerator.

WARNING

Take this icon seriously! Although the world won't end if you don't heed the advice next to this icon, the warnings are important to your success in preparing to take the GED test.

Where to Go from Here

Some people like to read books from beginning to end. Others prefer to read only the specific information they need to know now.

If you're a beginning-to-end type, you can start with Block 1 and proceed through each block sequentially. If you only want what you need to know now, I still suggest you start with Block 1, but then you can skip to whatever part of the book suits you best:

>> If you want to prepare for only one section of the GED, such as the Social Studies test, you can jump right to the social studies section in Block 2 and go from there.

>> If you want to test what you know first and then flip back to review what you missed, start with the shortened practice test in Block 4. Then check out Blocks 2 and 3 for help with areas you need to review.

Block 1

GED Overview in 20 Minutes

The GED test offers people without a high school diploma the opportunity to earn the equivalent of an American high school diploma without the need for full-time attendance in either day or night school. The GED test is a recognized standard that makes securing a job or starting college easier.

The recently revised test is in line with current Grade 12 standards in the United States and meets the College and Career Readiness Standards for Adult Education.

The GED test measures whether you understand what high school seniors across the country have studied before they graduate. Employers seek better-educated employees. Colleges want to make sure students are qualified. When you pass the GED test, you earn a high school equivalency diploma that can open many doors for you — perhaps doors that you don't even know exist at this point.

You may wonder why you should even bother taking the GED test and getting your GED diploma. One reason is that people with high school diplomas earn more and spend less time unemployed than people without diplomas. In a recent year, unemployment for people without a high school diploma was 5.9 percent. That dropped to 3.7 percent for individuals with a diploma or a GED certificate. Incomes were about 25 percent higher for high school or GED graduates than people without diplomas. In addition, your GED can qualify you for even more education. Earnings increase and unemployment decreases at each level of education from associate's degree on up. Even with just some college, you can earn more, on average.

Ready to get started? This block gives you the basics of the GED test: How the test is administered, what the test sections look like, how to schedule the test (and whether you're eligible), and how the scores are calculated (so you know what you need to pass).

Registering for the Test

Before you go online to sign up for the GED, you need to know a few things. After you determine that you're eligible, think about whether you want to take only one or two sections at a time or all sections at once. If you're eligible for accommodations, you need to have your documentation ready. The following sections walk you through the details.

Knowing if you're eligible

Before you schedule your test date, make sure that you meet the requirements to take the GED test. You're eligible to apply to take the GED test only if

>> **You're not currently enrolled in a high school.** If you're currently enrolled in a high school, you're expected to complete your diploma there. The purpose of the GED test is to give people who aren't in high school a chance to get an equivalent high school diploma.

>> **You're not a high school graduate.** If you're a high school graduate, you should have a diploma, which means you don't need to take the GED test.

>> **You meet state requirements regarding age, residency, and the length of time since leaving high school.** When you open your online account at https://ged.com, the software will screen you to ensure that you meet your state's requirements.

Choosing when and where to take the test

REMEMBER

You can take the GED when you're eligible and prepared. You can then apply to take the GED as soon as you want. Pick a day (or days) that works for you.

The GED has four sections: language arts, social studies, science, and math. You can take each of the four test sections separately, at different times, and in any order you want. Taking all four sections of the GED together takes about seven hours. However, the test is designed so you can take each section when you're ready. In fact, you can take the test sections one at a time, in the evenings or on weekends, depending on the individual testing center.

You can also take some of the tests online at home and others at a testing center. This flexibility is one of the benefits of doing the test by computer. If you want to take the test online at home, you must pass the GED Ready practice test before you can sign up. Even if you're taking the test at a test center, this short online test can help you determine whether you're likely to be successful, which can help you avoid wasting time and money on retests. And if you don't pass, the detailed feedback will help you find your strengths and areas for improvement.

As the time this book was published, some states don't offer the test and some don't allow online testing. You can take the test in a neighboring state that allows online or non-resident testing. Just select the state you'd like to test in when you set up your online account. This information changes periodically, so be sure to check https://ged.com/state-information-online-testing for the latest information. And remember: Nearly all employers and higher education schools nationally accept your passing score.

If you need special arrangements to accommodate your situation, the GED Testing Service will help arrange the test for you at a convenient time and location.

Asking for accommodations or language options

If you have a special need, it can be accommodated. You shouldn't feel bad about requesting an accommodation, either. Many people do, and the most common accommodations are for vision-related issues. Remember, though, that if you request an accommodation, you will need to provide acceptable documentation.

If you're learning English, you can choose to take the test in Spanish or, in Canada, French.

Disability accommodations

The GED Testing Service makes every effort to ensure that all qualified people have access to the tests. If you have a disability, you may not be able to register for the tests and take them the same week, but, with some advanced planning, you can probably take the tests when you're ready. Here's what you need to do:

>> Review the information and instructions at https://ged.com/about_test/accommodations.

>> At least a month before you want to take the test, go to https://ged.com and open an online account, or log into an existing account.

>> Follow the instructions to request an accommodation. The software will walk you through the steps to request an accommodation and submit the proper documentation.

>> You will need documentation of your special need from an appropriate professional. The software will give the exact requirements and instructions you can show the professional so they can provide the correct documentation.

>> Complete all the proper forms and submit them with a medical or professional diagnosis.

>> Start planning early so that you're able to take the tests when you're ready.

The GED Testing Service defines specific disabilities, such as the following, for which it may make special accommodations:

>> Learning and cognitive disorders (LCD)

>> Attention deficit/hyperactivity disorder (ADHD)

>> Psychological and psychiatric disorders (EPP)

>> Physical disabilities and chronic health conditions (PCH)

Language options

The good news is that English doesn't have to be your first language for you to take the GED test. In the United States, the GED test is offered in English and Spanish. A French version is available in Canada.

TIP

If English (or Spanish) isn't your first language, you must decide whether you can read and write English or Spanish as well as or better than 40 percent of high school graduates. If so, then you can prepare for and take the test without additional language preparation. If you don't read or write English or Spanish well enough to pass, then you need to take additional classes to improve your language skills until you think you're ready. Your local community college or adult education center is the best place to get started. Your account at https://ged.com can also help you find local programs that will suit your needs.

Signing up for your test

You book your appointment through the GED Testing Service's website, https://ged.com, based on available testing dates. When you sign up for the test, you can search for times and locations that suit you. Because a computer administers the test, you will schedule an individual appointment. Your test starts when you start and ends when the allotted time ends.

If you sign up to take the test online at home, your computer and your home (or other location where you take the test) have to meet special requirements outlined when you sign up. The https://ged.com website will walk you through these requirements. If you sign up to take the test at a testing center, you will take the test in a computer lab, often containing no more than 15 seats; testing facilities may be located in many communities in your state.

Identifying What to Bring to the Test

Passing the GED can bring you many benefits, so you need to treat it seriously and come prepared. Make sure you bring the following items with you on test day:

» **You:** The most important thing to bring to the GED test is obviously you. If you enroll to take the test, you have to show up; otherwise, you'll receive a big fat zero and lose your testing fee. If something unfortunate happens after you enroll, go to your online account and see if you can reschedule. You may need to call the GED Testing Service or use their online chat to reschedule.

» **Correct identification:** Before you can start the test, the test proctors — online and in person — want to make sure that you're really you. Bring a government-issued photo ID — a driver's license, a state ID card, a passport, or a matrícula consular are all fine. Have your ID in a place where you can easily reach it. And, when asked to identify yourself, don't pull out a mirror and say, "Yep, that's me."

» **Registration confirmation:** The registration confirmation is your proof that you did register. If you're taking the test in an area where everybody knows you and everything you do, you may not need the confirmation, but I suggest you take it anyway. It's light and doesn't take up much room in your pocket or purse.

» **Other miscellaneous items:** After you register for the test, you receive instructions that list what you need to bring with you. Besides yourself and the items I listed previously, other items you want to bring or wear include the following:

- **Comfortable clothes and shoes.** When you're taking the test, you want to be as relaxed as possible. Uncomfortable clothes and shoes may distract you from doing your best. You're taking the GED test, not modeling the most recent fashions.

- **A bottle of water and a healthful snack.** Check whether you can bring these with you into the room at the testing center. If you test online at home, you are only allowed to have some water, in a clear glass, on the desk with you. But you can eat a quick snack in the 10-minute break between tests if you take more than one test.

- **Reading glasses.** If you need glasses to read a computer monitor, don't forget to bring them to the test. Bring a spare pair, if you have one. You can't do the test if you can't read the screen.

- **Calculator.** You may bring a handheld Texas Instruments TI-30XS MultiView calculator to the testing center, which you may use whenever the calculator icon appears on the screen. For many people, a real calculator saves time on the test. However, you aren't required to BYOC (bring your own calculator). A calculator icon appears on the screen whenever one is necessary to answer a question. All you have to do is click on the calculator icon, and you have a fully functioning calculator on-screen. See the section "On-screen calculator" later in this block for details about how to use it.

Knowing What to Expect During the Test

When you know what to expect during the GED, it's easier to do your best on the test. The following section explains what you need to know: the exam room rules, the computer skills you need, and an overview of the material you need to know for each section of the GED.

Understanding exam room rules

The rules about what enters the testing room are strict. Don't take any chances. If something isn't on the list of acceptable items and isn't normal clothing, leave it at home. Laptops, cellphones, and other electronic devices will most likely be banned from the testing area.

Leave other electronics at home, locked in your car, or in a locker at the testing center. The last place on earth to discuss whether you can bring something into the test site is at the door on test day.

REMEMBER

Whatever you do, be sure *not* to bring the following with you to the testing room at the GED testing center, and make sure they are out of reach (or out of the room) if you test at home:

>> Books

>> Notes or scratch paper

>> Tablets

>> Cellphones

>> Smartwatches

>> Apple AirPods or other wireless earphones

>> Anything valuable, like a laptop computer that you don't feel comfortable leaving outside the room while you take the test

Also, keep your eyes on your monitor. Everybody knows not to look at other people's work during the test, but, to be on the safe side, don't stretch, roll your eyes, or do anything else that may be mistaken for looking at another test. At a test center, most of the tests will be different on the various computers, so looking around is futile and doing so can get you into a lot of trouble. You should also keep your eyes on the screen if you test online at home. Everything you need to take the test is on the screen in front of you. Looking around the room or looking away from the screen repeatedly could be considered suspicious behavior.

Identifying computer skills you need

If you know how to use a computer and are comfortable with a keyboard and a mouse, you're ahead of the game. If not, practice your keyboarding. Also, practice reading from a computer screen because reading from a screen is very different from reading printed materials. At the very least, you need to get more comfortable with computers, even if that means taking a short course at a local learning emporium. In the case of the GED test, the more familiar you are with computers, the more comfortable you'll feel taking the test.

When taking the computerized GED test, you have two important tools to allow you to answer questions: the keyboard and the mouse. You may also use an on-screen calculator and whiteboard for certain parts of the test. The following sections examine each tool in greater depth and explain exactly how you use them to complete the GED test. Make sure that you understand the mechanics and use of the keyboard and mouse beforehand so you don't waste valuable time figuring out all of this stuff on test day.

Typing on the keyboard

You need to have at least some familiarity with a computer's keyboard. If you constantly make typing errors or aren't familiar with the keyboard, you may be in trouble. The good news is that you don't have to be a keyboarding whiz. In fact, the behind-the-scenes GED people have shown through their research that even people with minimal keyboarding skills still have adequate time to complete the test.

On the GED test, you'll use the keyboard to type your answers in the essay (Extended Response) segment in the Reasoning through Language Arts test and in the fill-in-the-blank questions on the other three tests. These answers can include words, phrases, and numbers. Although you may be familiar with typing by using one or two fingers on your smartphone or tablet, with the screen often predicting and suggesting (correctly spelled) words that you need, the word processor on the GED test for the Extended Response has a bare minimum of features. It accepts keyboard entries, cuts, pastes, and copies and lets you redo and undo changes, but no more. It doesn't have a grammar-checker or a spell-checker, so be careful with your keyboarding because spelling and grammatical errors are just that — errors.

TIP

The GED test uses the standard English keyboard (see Figure 1-1). If you're not familiar with it, take time to acquaint yourself with it before you take the GED test. If you're used to other language keyboards, you will find that the English keyboard has some letters and punctuation that appear in different places. Before test day, practice using the English keyboard so that the differences in the keyboard don't throw you off the day of the test. You won't have time to figure out the keyboard while the clock is ticking.

FIGURE 1-1:
An example of
a standard
English
keyboard.

© John Wiley & Sons, Inc.

Clicking and dragging with the mouse

Most questions on the GED test require no more than the ability to use the mouse to move the cursor on your screen to point to a selection for your answer and then click that selection, which is very basic.

If you're unfamiliar with computers, take time to become familiar with the mouse, including the clickable buttons and the scroll wheel. If the mouse has a scroll wheel, you can use it to move up or down through text or images. When you hold down the left button on the mouse, it highlights text as you drag the cursor across the screen, or you can "drag and drop" questions on the screen.

If you test online at home using a laptop, that computer may have a trackpad mouse (a small panel at the bottom of the screen that you touch with one or more fingers to move the pointer on-screen and click in the left or right corner). Use the instructions that come with your laptop to get familiar with a trackpad mouse. If you're more comfortable with a traditional mouse, you can buy a wired or wireless one for a few dollars online. Make sure that it's compatible with your specific laptop.

FINDING HELP WITH COMPUTER SKILLS

Some websites offer free training on basic computer skills, but you need a computer to use them. Your local library should have free computer access if you don't have your own computer. Many libraries and community agencies offer free computer classes that are worth checking out. If you're a bit computer savvy, type "basic computer skills training + free" into a search engine and follow the links until you find one that suits you. If you want to improve your typing skills, search online in your favorite search engine using the keywords "free typing tutor." Be aware that free or limited-time trial software can be full of advertising.

Take your time at home or in the library developing your skills and working through the practice tests. Test day isn't the time to figure out how to use the computer.

On the GED test, you'll use the mouse or keyboard to answer the four main question types: multiple-choice, fill-in-the-blank, drop-down menu, and drag-and-drop. You'll use both the mouse and the keyboard to answer the Extended Response item on the RLA test.

Fill-in-the-blanks are another type of question you'll encounter on the GED test. They're simply statements with a blank box in the text somewhere. To answer the question, you need to enter the word(s), name, or number. The statement will be preceded by directions setting up the text, so you'll know what is expected.

REMEMBER

You must type the precise word or number required. Spelling mistakes, misplaced decimals, and even wrong capitalization count as errors.

Calculating with the on-screen calculator

The Math test provides an on-screen calculator for you to use on all but the first five questions of the test. (If you don't see the calculator tab on the screen, then you have to do the math in your head or on the whiteboard.) When you need the calculator, simply click on the Calculator link and the calculator appears (see Figure 1-2). If you test at a testing center, you can bring your own TI-30XS MultiView calculator. The GED Testing Service's website, https://ged.com, has a number of resources, including a reference sheet that shows you all the features you need to know and an actual on-screen calculator you can practice with.

Using the tablet or on-screen whiteboard

You don't get scratch paper when you take the GED. Instead, you have an erasable tablet and/or on-screen whiteboard for taking notes about your essay, solving math problems, and so on. If you take the test at a testing center, you'll have an erasable tablet. If you test at a testing center or online at home, you'll have an online whiteboard for taking notes and organizing your ideas. Either way, nothing you write on the boards will be seen by anyone but you. Only the answer that you enter in the answer window counts.

The order, topics, and time for each test

The GED test includes the four sections (also referred to as tests) outlined in Table 1-1. Each test is timed and covers somewhat predictable topics, also outlined in Table 1-1 and covered in the following sections. For help preparing for each of these tests, see Block 2 for background information and Block 3 for sample questions.

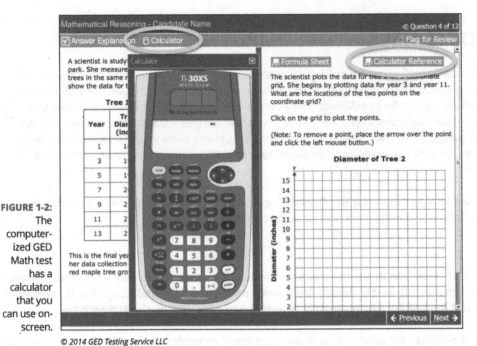

FIGURE 1-2: The computerized GED Math test has a calculator that you can use on-screen.

© 2014 GED Testing Service LLC

TABLE 1-1   Time for Each GED Test Section

Test Section	Time Limit (in Minutes)
Reasoning through Language Arts	95 (split into two sections, 35 and 60)
Reasoning through Language Arts, Extended Response	45
Social Studies	70
Science	90
Mathematical Reasoning	115

Reasoning through the Language Arts test

The Reasoning through Language Arts (RLA) test is one long test that covers all the literacy components of the GED test. You have 150 minutes overall. However, the test is divided into three sections:

>> The Reading Comprehension section is 35 minutes and asks you to demonstrate a critical understanding of various passages.

>> The Extended Response (essay) is 45 minutes, followed by a 10-minute break. This test examines your skills in organizing your thoughts and writing clearly.

>> The Grammar and Language section is 60 minutes and asks you to correct errors in various kinds of texts. This includes demonstrating a command of proper grammar, punctuation, and spelling.

Remember that the time for the Extended Response can't be used to work on the other questions in the test, nor can you use leftover time from the other sections on the Extended Response.

The scores from all three components will be combined into one single score for the RLA test.

The question-answer part of this test consists mainly of various types of multiple-choice questions and drop-down menu questions with four answer choices. You'll also see drag-and-drop questions.

The questions are based on source texts, which are materials presented to you for your response. Some of this source material is nonfiction, from science and social studies content as well as from the workplace. Only 25 percent is based on literature. Here's a breakdown of the materials:

>> **Workplace and community materials:** These include work-related letters, memos, and instructions that you may see on the job. They also include letters and documents from companies and community organizations, such as banks, hospitals, libraries, credit unions, and local governments.

>> **U.S. founding documents and documents that present part of the Great American Conversation:** These may include extracts from the Bill of Rights, the Constitution, and other historical documents. They also may include opinion pieces on relevant issues in American history and civics.

>> **Informational works:** These include documents that present information (often dry and boring information), such as an instructional manual. They also include materials that you may find in history, social studies, or science books.

>> **Literature:** These include extracts from novels and short stories.

Social Studies test

On the Social Studies test, you have 70 minutes to answer 50 questions. On this test, you will see standard multiple-choice questions, as well as fill-in-the-blank questions, drag-and-drop questions, and drop-down menu questions. A few questions may ask you to calculate an answer.

The questions are based on various kinds of source texts. About half of the questions are based on one source text, such as a graph or short reading, with one question. Other questions have a single source text as the basis for several questions. In either case, you'll need to analyze and evaluate the content presented to you as part of the question. A few questions may ask you to compare and contrast information from two different sources. The test questions evaluate your ability to use reasoning and analysis skills. The information for the source materials comes from primary and secondary sources, both text and visual. That means you need to be able to "read" and interpret tables, maps, and graphs as well as standard text materials.

The content of the Social Studies test is drawn from the following four basic areas:

>> **Civics and government:** The largest part (about 50 percent of the test) focuses on civics and government. The civics and government questions examine the development of democracy, from ancient times to present day. Other topics include how civilizations change over time and respond to crises.

>> **American history:** American history makes up 20 percent of the test. It covers all topics from the pilgrims and early settlement to the Revolution, the Civil War, World Wars I and II, the Vietnam War, and current history — all of which involve the United States in one way or another.

>> **Economics:** Economics makes up about 15 percent of the test. The economics portion examines basic theories, such as supply and demand, the role of government policies in the economy, and macro- and microeconomic theory.

>> **Geography and the world:** This area also makes up 15 percent of the test. The areas with which you need to become familiar are very topical: sustainability and environmental issues, population issues, and rural and urban settlement. Other topics include cultural diversity and migration.

A good way to prepare for this test is to read as much as possible. As you prepare for the test, read articles about civics, history, economics, and geography from reliable online sources. Even reading solid news coverage can help you develop the strong reading skills you need.

Science test

The Science test is scheduled for 90 minutes. My advice for the Science test is the same as for the Reasoning through Language Arts test: Read as much as you can, especially science material. Whenever you don't understand a word or concept, look it up in a dictionary or online. The questions in the Science test assume a high school level of science vocabulary.

You don't have to be a nuclear physicist to answer the questions, but you should be familiar with the vocabulary normally understood by someone completing high school. If you work at improving your scientific vocabulary, you should have little trouble with the Science test. (*Note:* That same advice applies to all the GED test's sections. Improve your vocabulary in each subject and you'll perform better.)

The Science test concentrates on two main themes:

>> Human health and living systems

>> Energy and related systems

In addition, the content of the test focuses on the following areas:

>> **Physical science:** About 40 percent of the test focuses on physics and chemistry, including topics such as conservation, transformation, and flow of energy; work, motion, and forces; and chemical properties and reactions related to living systems.

>> **Life science:** Another 40 percent of the Science test deals with life science, including biology and, more specifically, human body and health, the relationship between life functions and energy intake, ecosystems, structure and function of life, and the molecular basis for heredity and evolution.

>> **Earth and space science:** This area makes up the remaining 20 percent of this test and includes astronomy — interaction between Earth's systems and living things, Earth and its system components and interactions, and structure and organization of the cosmos.

Go ahead and type one of the three areas of content into your favorite search engine to find material to read. You'll find links to articles and material from all different levels. Filter your choices by the level you want and need — for example, use keywords such as "scientific theories," "scientific discoveries," "scientific method," "human health," "living systems," "energy," "the universe," "organisms," and "geochemical systems" — and don't get discouraged if you can't understand technical material that one scientist wrote that only about three other scientists in the world can understand.

The questions on the Science test are in multiple-choice, fill-in-the-blank, drag-and-drop, and drop-down menu formats. As on the Social Studies test, you will read passages and interpret graphs, tables, and other visual materials. A few questions may ask you to calculate an answer.

Mathematical Reasoning test

The Mathematical Reasoning (Math) test checks that you have the same knowledge and understanding of mathematics as a typical high school graduate. Because the GED is designed to prepare you for both postsecondary education and employment, it has an emphasis on both workplace-related mathematics and academic mathematics. About 45 percent of the test is about quantitative problem solving, and the rest is about algebra.

The Math test consists of different question formats to be completed in 115 minutes. Because the GED test is administered on the computer, the questions take advantage of the power of the computer. Some questions will simply pose a problem for you to solve. Other questions will refer to various kinds of stimulus materials, including graphs, tables, menus, price lists, and much more.

On the Math test, most of the questions are multiple choice with four answer choices. You'll also see a few drop-down questions and drag-and-drop questions, which typically ask you to arrange numbers in a certain order by clicking and dragging them on-screen. Fill-in-the-blank questions ask you to type your answer as a specific number or word into the space provided.

Some questions may be stand-alone with only one question for each stimulus. Others may have multiple questions based on a single stimulus. Each stimulus, no matter how many questions are based on it, may include text, graphs, tables, or some other representation of numeric, geometrical, or algebraic materials. Practice reading mathematical materials and become familiar with the vocabulary of mathematics. On the Math test, you're allowed to use your calculator on all but the first five questions. However, some questions can be answered more quickly using mental math or simple calculations on the whiteboard.

Navigating the question types

The GED has four types of questions. Before you take the test, have a look at each type and make sure you understand how to answer it on the computerized test.

Multiple-choice questions

In all the GED tests, the multiple-choice question is the most common. The basic multiple-choice question, shown in Figure 1-3, looks very similar to what you may expect. This one is presented in split-screen form, with the source text on the left and the question and answer choices on the right. If the source text extends beyond one screen, you use the scroll bar on the right side of the left screen. When you're ready to answer, use the mouse to click on the appropriate answer, and then click on Next to continue.

REMEMBER

If a scroll bar accompanies the source text on the left side of the screen, some of the text isn't visible unless you scroll down. If that scroll bar is on the answer side, some of the answer choices may not be visible without scrolling. This is important to remember because you may miss some important text when trying to answer the question. To use the scroll bar, click it with your cursor and then move your mouse up or down. When the text you want is visible, release the button.

Drag-and-drop questions

Figure 1-4 shows a drag-and-drop question. This question uses a four-page source text and asks you to select characteristics that apply to the main character, Anne. The key is that you can select only three of the five listed words. That isn't stated in the question but is obvious from the drag-and-drop targets, which include only three oval spaces. You have to read the text carefully to find the correct choices. When you decide which words apply, drag each word to one of the ovals and leave it there. Click on Next to continue.

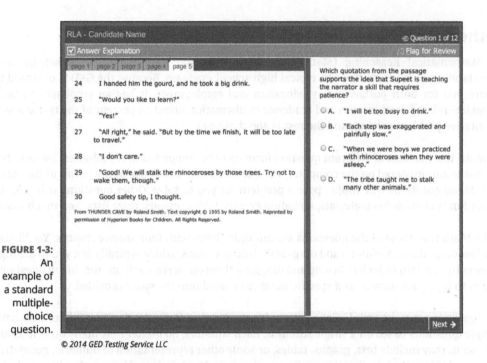

FIGURE 1-3:
An example of a standard multiple-choice question.

© 2014 GED Testing Service LLC

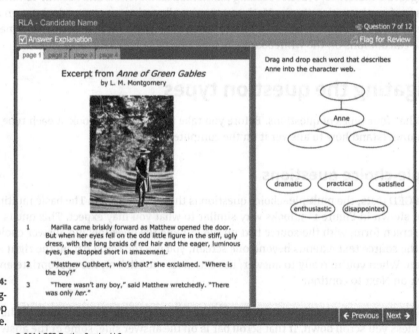

FIGURE 1-4:
A drag-and-drop example.

© 2014 GED Testing Service LLC

Drop-down menu questions

Questions involving a drop-down menu (see Figure 1-5) are just a variation of the multiple-choice questions. You use the mouse to expand the choices and then again to select the correct one.

Fill-in-the-blank questions

For fill-in-the-blank questions, you type an answer in a box provided, using the keyboard. The answer might be a word or phrase, a number, or an equation. On the math test, you may have to use the symbols on the keyboard or click on the Æ Symbol tab for additional symbols that you may need (see Figure 1-6).

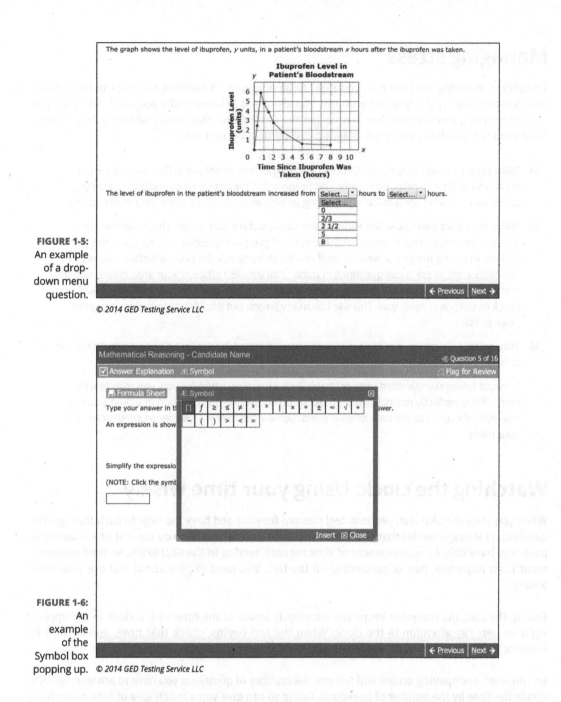

The graph shows the level of ibuprofen, *y* units, in a patient's bloodstream *x* hours after the ibuprofen was taken.

Ibuprofen Level in Patient's Bloodstream

The level of ibuprofen in the patient's bloodstream increased from Select... ▾ hours to Select... ▾ hours.

Select...
0
2/3
2 1/2
5
8

← Previous | Next →

FIGURE 1-5:
An example of a drop-down menu question.

© 2014 GED Testing Service LLC

Mathematical Reasoning - Candidate Name ⏱ Question 5 of 16

☑ Answer Explanation   Æ Symbol   ⚐ Flag for Review

🔲 Formula Sheet   Æ Symbol   ☒

Type your answer in t[...] [symbols] [...]swer.

An expression is show[...]

Simplify the expressio[...]

(NOTE: Click the sym[...]

Insert ☒ Close

← Previous | Next →

FIGURE 1-6:
An example of the Symbol box popping up.

© 2014 GED Testing Service LLC

After reading the question carefully, you use the keyboard and the Symbol box to type your answer in the box. To insert a symbol, place your cursor in the correct place in the answer box. Then click on the Æ Symbol tab. The Symbol box will open. In the Symbol box, click on the symbol you want and then click the Insert button in the lower-right corner of the Symbol box. The symbol will appear next to your cursor. To make the Symbol box go away, press the Close button in the lower-right corner.

Discovering Important Test-Taking Strategies

You can increase your score by mastering a few smart test-taking strategies. To help you do so, I give you some tips in these sections on managing stress, managing your time, and answering questions.

Managing stress

To succeed in taking the GED test, you need to be prepared. In addition to studying the content and skills needed for the four test sections, you also want to be mentally prepared. Although you may be nervous, you can't let your nerves get the best of you. Stay calm and take a deep breath. Here are a few pointers to help you stay focused on the task at hand:

>> **Take time to relax.** Passing the GED test is an important milestone in life. Make sure you leave a bit of time to relax, both while you prepare for the test sections and just before you take them. Relaxing has a place in preparing as long as it doesn't become your main activity.

>> **Make sure that you know the rules of the room before you begin.** The earlier section, "Exam room rules," explains most of these rules. If you have questions about using the bathroom during the test or what to do if you finish early, ask the proctor before you begin. If you don't want to ask these questions in public, call the GED office in your area before test day, and ask your questions over the telephone. For general GED questions, call 877-392-6433 or check out https://ged.com. This site has many pages, but the FAQ page is always a good place to start.

>> **Stay calm.** Your nerves can use up a lot of energy needed for the test. Concentrate on the job at hand. You can always be nervous or panicky some other time.

Because taking standardized tests probably isn't a usual situation for you, you may feel nervous. This is perfectly normal. Just try to focus on answering one question at a time and push any other thoughts to the back of your mind. Sometimes taking a few deep breaths can clear your mind.

Watching the clock: Using your time wisely

When you start the GED test, you may feel pressed for time and have the urge to rush through the questions. I strongly advise that you don't. You have sufficient time to do the test at a reasonable pace. You have only a certain amount of time for each section in the GED exam, so time management is an important part of succeeding on the test. You need to plan ahead and use your time wisely.

During the test, the computer keeps you constantly aware of the time with a clock in the upper-right corner. Pay attention to the clock. When the test begins, check that time, and be sure to monitor how much time you have left as you work your way through the test.

TIP

As you start, the opening screen will tell you the number of questions you have to answer. Quickly divide the time by the number of questions. Doing so can give you a rough idea of how much time to spend on each question. For example, on the Mathematical Reasoning test, suppose that you have 50 questions to answer. You have 115 minutes to complete the test. Divide the time by the number of questions to find out how much time you have for each one: 115/50 = 2.3 minutes or 2 minutes and 18 seconds per question. As you progress, repeat the calculation to see how you're doing.

TIP

Remember that you can answer the questions in any order, except for the RLA Extended Response. Do the easiest questions first. If you come to a question that will take a long time to answer (such as a complicated math question), skip it. If you get stuck on a question, leave it and come back to it later if you have time. If you are unsure of an answer, use the Flag for Review button to mark it so you can return to it later if you have time. The Review screen will help you quickly find and return to flagged and skipped questions later in the test. In the meantime, you can keep to that schedule and answer as many questions as possible.

The following general time-management tips to help you complete each exam on time:

>> **Measure the time you have to answer each question without spending more time on timing than answering.** Group questions together; for example, calculate how much time you have for each question on each test. Multiply the answer by 5 to give you a time slot for any five test questions. Then try to make sure that you answer each group of five questions within the time you've calculated. Doing so helps you complete all the questions and leaves you several minutes for review.

>> **Keep calm and don't panic.** The time you spend panicking could be better spent answering questions.

>> **Practice using the sample test in this book and the online-only test.** The more you practice timed sample test questions, the easier managing a timed test becomes. You can get used to doing something in a limited amount of time if you practice. Block 4 is a shortened practice test.

When time is up, immediately stop and breathe a sigh of relief. When the test ends, the examiner will give you a log-off procedure. Listen for instructions on what to do or where to go next.

Addressing and answering questions

When you start the test, you want to have a game plan in place for how to answer the questions. Keep the following tips in mind to help you address each question:

>> **Whenever you read a question, ask yourself, "What am I being asked?"** Doing so helps you stay focused on what you need to find out to answer the question. Then try to answer it.

>> **Try to eliminate some answers.** Even if you don't really know the answer, the process of elimination can help. When you're offered four answer choices, some will be obviously wrong. Eliminate those choices, and you improve your odds of guessing a correct answer.

>> **Don't overthink.** Because all the questions are straightforward, don't look for trick questions. The questions ask for an answer based on the information given.

>> **Find the best answer and quickly verify that it answers the question.** If it does, click on that choice and move on. If it doesn't, leave it and come back to it after you answer all the other questions, if you have time. *Remember:* You need to pick the *most* correct answer from the choices offered. It may not be the perfect answer, but it is what is required.

Guess for success: Using intelligent guessing

The multiple-choice questions, regardless of the on-screen format, provide you with four possible answers. You get between one and three points for every correct answer. Nothing is subtracted for incorrect answers. That means you can guess on the questions you don't know for sure without fear that you'll lose points. Make educated guesses by eliminating as many obviously wrong choices as possible and choosing from just one or two remaining choices.

Removing one or two choices you know are wrong makes choosing the correct answer much more likely. For example, if you know that two of the answers are wrong, you leave yourself only two possible answers to choose from, giving you a 50 percent (1 in 2) chance of guessing right — much better than 25 percent!

Try to spot the wrong choices by following these tips:

>> **Make sure that the answer choice really answers the question.** Wrong choices usually don't answer the question — that is, they may sound good, but they answer a different question than the one the test asks.

>> **When two answer choices seem very close, consider both of them carefully because they both can't be right — but they both *can* be wrong.** Some answer choices may be very close, and all seem correct, but there's a fine line between completely correct and nearly correct. Be careful. These answer choices are sometimes given to see whether you really understand the material.

>> **Look for opposite answers in the hopes that you can eliminate one.** If two answers contradict each other, both can't be right, but both can be wrong.

>> **Trust your instincts.** Some wrong choices may just strike you as wrong when you first read them. If you spend time preparing for the test, you probably know more than you think.

Leaving time for review

Having a few minutes at the end of a test to check your work is a great way to set your mind at ease. As soon as you answer the last question, the test will take you to the Review screen, which will show you a list of all the questions, and whether you skipped or flagged any questions. This way, you can quickly review any questions that may be troubling and go back and answer any ones you skipped earlier. Keep the following tips in mind as you review your answers:

>> **Figure out how much time you have per remaining question, and try to answer each question in a little less than that time.** The extra seconds you don't use the first time through the test add up to time at the end of the test for review. Some questions require more thought and decision-making than others. Use your extra seconds to answer those questions.

>> **Don't change a lot of answers at the last minute.** Second-guessing yourself can lead to trouble. Often, second-guessing leads you to changing correct answers to incorrect ones. Numerous studies show that when a test-taker changes an answer selection, the new selection is usually incorrect. If you have prepared well and worked numerous sample questions, then you're likely to get the correct answers the first time. Ignoring all your preparation and knowledge to play a hunch isn't a good idea, either at the racetrack or on a test.

>> **If you cannot answer all the questions in the time remaining, answer them randomly.** There is no guessing penalty on the GED, so don't leave any questions unanswered. The one or two points you pick up from answering all the questions may be the points you need to pass.

>> **On the Extended Response section, use any remaining time to reread and review your final essay.** You may have written a good essay, but you always need to check for typos and grammar mistakes. The essay is evaluated for style, content, and proper English. That includes spelling and grammar.

The Flag for Review button is a very useful feature on all four tests. This button allows you to mark questions for review later. You can select an answer and then press Flag for Review, or simply press Flag for Review without selecting an answer. At the end of the test, or at any time, you can go to the Review screen, which shows all the questions that are flagged or skipped. This way, you can return to these questions quickly at any time. When you complete the test, you will also be taken to this screen (as long as there is time remaining). You can continue to check your answers or complete unanswered questions until time runs out.

Understanding Your Score

To pass, you need to score a minimum of 145 on each section of the test, and you must pass each section of the test to earn your GED diploma. If you achieve a passing score, congratulate yourself: You've scored better than at least 40 percent of today's high school graduates, and you're now a graduate of the largest virtual school in the country. And if your scores range between 165 and 174, you've reached the GED College Ready level. This means you may be able to start your college studies right away without any additional college-readiness classes. This can save you time and money. If your scores are even higher, between 175 and 200, you've reached the lofty GED College Ready + Credit level. Depending on the policies of your institution, you can qualify for college credit in each of the GED subject areas.

TIP

If you score at the College-Ready or College Ready + Credit level, shop around at various colleges and universities. Some institutions may be more willing than others to waive requirements or grant credit. For example, you can start at a community college that grants credit. Then those credits will be on your transcript if you later go on to a four-year college.

There is more good news. Scores from the computer-based and online tests do not expire, so if you passed some sections years ago, you do not need to take them again. And if you took a test between 2014 and 2016 and scored below 150 but above 145, you will now get credit for passing that section of the test. (The passing score was lowered from 150 to 145 at that time.) Your transcript should have been adjusted automatically, so check your transcript at https://ged.com; there may be good news waiting for you. The following sections address a few more points you may want to know about how the GED test is scored and what you can do if you score poorly on some or all of the test sections.

Identifying how scores are determined

Correct answers may be worth one, two, or more points, depending on the question and the level of difficulty. The Extended Response (also known as the essay) is scored separately. However, the Extended Response is only one part of the Reasoning through Language Arts test. On each test section, you must accumulate a minimum of 145 points.

Retaking a test to improve your score

If you discover that your score is less than 145 on any test section, start planning to retake the test(s) — and make sure you leave plenty of time for additional studying and preparing.

TIP

As soon as possible after seeing your results, check out the rules for retaking that section of the test at https://ged.com. Remember, you need to retake only those sections of the test that you didn't pass. Any sections you pass are completed and count toward your diploma. Furthermore, the detailed feedback you receive on your results will help you discover areas that need more work before retaking a section of the test. That information can help you determine the sections of this book to review or whether you want to sign up for a class. You can find nearby adult education centers on https://ged.com.

No matter what score you receive on your first round of the section, don't be afraid to retake any section that you didn't pass. After you've taken it once, you know what you need to work on, and you know exactly what to expect on test day. Just take a deep breath and get ready to prepare some more before you take your next test.

Block 2

Preparing for the Test

To be ready for the GRE, you need to know what's on the test and get some tips for responding for the seemingly endless questions you must answer in a short amount of time. In other words, this block helps you put on your game face before you walk into the exam room. You'll know what you need to know, or if you're not sure of the answers, you'll have some strategies for getting through it.

Exploring the Language Arts Test

The Reasoning through Language Arts (RLA) test evaluates your ability to do the following:

>> Apply skills in reading comprehension.

>> Apply writing skills to create a logical and effective extended response (essay).

>> Apply concepts in grammar and language to correct errors in writing. *Grammar* is *the* basic structure of language — you know: subjects, verbs, sentences, fragments, and all that. *Language* includes vocabulary, usage, punctuation, capitalization, and other features of written English.

Most of what you're tested on the RLA test is stuff that you've picked up over the years, either in school or just by speaking, reading, and observing. However, to help you prepare better for this test, I give you some more skill-building tips in this block.

Choosing wisely in the reading component

In today's society, being able to comprehend, analyze, and apply something you've read is the strongest predictor of career and college readiness and an important skill set to have. In the following sections, you explore the four aspects of good reading skills: comprehension, analysis, command of evidence, and synthesis.

The RLA test Reading Comprehension component consists of excerpts from fiction and nonfiction prose. You're presented with a reading passage (or in some cases, two related reading passages) followed by a series of multiple-choice and drag-and-drop questions.

Understanding types of reading comprehension questions

The questions on the RLA reading portion of the test focus on the following skills, which you're expected to be able to use as you read both fiction and nonfiction passages.

» **Comprehension:** Questions that test your *comprehension* skills assess your ability to do close reading — that is, to read a source of information thoughtfully so that you have a precise understanding of what you've read and can restate the information in your own words. Items may also ask you to show understanding by ordering events in a passage or to rephrase what you read without losing the meaning of the passage. In addition, items can ask you to show how the details support the main idea. Other items ask you to determine the meaning of specific words in context and grasp how a writer's use of a particular word or phrase affects the meaning of a sentence, a paragraph, or the entire passage.

» **Analysis:** Questions that test your *analysis* skills assess your ability to draw conclusions, understand consequences, and make inferences about the passage. To answer these questions, make sure your answers are based only on the information in the passage and not on outside knowledge or the online article you read last week. Items may ask you to explain how parts of the passage (such as paragraphs, sentences, and examples) work together to accomplish the writer's purpose. Other items may ask you to show how transitional words and phrases (such as *however* and *for example*) signal relationships among ideas in the passage. Other items may ask you to analyze the writer's purposes in writing the passage — to convince, to share knowledge with the reader, or even to amuse the reader!

» **Command of evidence:** These questions assess your ability to identify and evaluate evidence. You need to understand the passage writer's point of view in order to assess the strength and weakness of their position. Some questions will ask you to identify the evidence that the author uses for support. Other times, you will have to identify among the options additional supporting evidence. Other questions will ask you whether the author's evidence offers valid support for a position, or merely an opinion or belief unsupported by reasons, examples, or facts.

» **Synthesis:** Questions that test your *synthesis* skills assess your ability to take information in one form and in one location and put it together with information in another context. Here, you get a chance to make connections between two related passages and compare and contrast them. You may be asked to compare and contrast the tone, point of view, style, effectiveness, or purposes of the passages — and saying that the purpose of a passage is to confuse and confound test-takers isn't the answer!

REMEMBER

Some reading questions may ask you to use information in the source text passages combined with information presented in the questions. So make sure you use all the information that you have available. And don't forget to use the tabs and scroll bars to reveal the complete passage and question — you never know where an answer may come from.

Developing skills to read well

To succeed on the RLA test, you can prepare in advance by improving your reading skills. Here are some of the best ways you can prepare:

» **Read as often as you can.** This strategy is the best one and is by far the simplest, because reading exposes you to correct grammar. What you read makes a difference. Reading catalogs may increase your product knowledge and improve your research skills, but reading literature is preferable because it introduces you to so many rules of grammar. Reading fiction exposes you to interesting words and sentences. It shows you how paragraphs tie into one another and how each paragraph has a topic and generally sticks to it. Reading historical fiction can give you some insight into what led up to today and can also help you with the Social Studies test (discussed later in this block).

Reading nonfiction — from instructions to business letters, from press releases to history books and historical documents — is also extremely important. Nonfiction generally uses a formal style, the kind expected of you when you write an essay for the Extended Response item. Older documents can be a special problem because the writing style is very different from what's common today. Getting familiar with such documents will help you get better results and even help with your Social Studies test.

TIP

Read everything you can get your hands on — even cereal boxes — and identify what kind of reading you're doing. Read about topics that interest you, which can include subjects as varied as new cars, sports reporting, healthcare news, or money-saving tips. Reading aloud to your children at bedtime also counts and so does reading on your phone while you are on the bus or waiting to see your doctor. Ask yourself questions about your reading and see how much of it you can remember.

>> **Develop your reading speed.** Reading is wonderful, but reading quickly is even better — it gets you through the test with time to spare. Do a quick Internet search to find plenty of material that can help you read faster. Whatever method you use, try to improve your reading rate without hurting your overall reading comprehension.

>> **Read carefully.** When you read, read carefully and think about what you're reading. This is called *active reading:* Your brain is working as hard as your eyes are. If reading novels, stories, or historical documents is unfamiliar to you, read these items even more carefully and thoughtfully. The more carefully you read any material, the easier it'll be for you to get the right answers on the test.

>> **Ask questions.** Ask yourself questions about what you read. Could you take a newspaper article and reduce the content to four bulleted points and still summarize the article accurately? Do you understand the main ideas well enough to explain them to a stranger?

Ask for help if you don't understand something that you read. You may want to form a study group and work with other people. If you're taking a test-preparation course, ask the instructor for help when you need it. If you have family, friends, or coworkers who can help, ask them.

>> **Use a dictionary.** Not many people understand every word they read, so use a dictionary. There are many good free or inexpensive dictionary apps for your computer or smartphone. Looking up unfamiliar words increases your vocabulary, which, in turn, makes passages on the Reasoning through Language Arts test easier to understand. If you have a thesaurus, use it, too. Often, knowing a synonym for the word you don't know is helpful. Plus, it improves your Scrabble game!

>> **Use new words.** A new word doesn't usually become part of your vocabulary until you put it to use in your everyday language. When you come across a new word, make sure you know its meaning and try to use it in a sentence. Then try to work it into conversation for a day or two. After a while, this challenge can make each day more exciting. If you don't know what you don't know, then you can find lists of important words online, such as "the 100 most commonly misspelled or misunderstood words" or "words important to pass the GED." These can be a good start to increasing your vocabulary.

REMEMBER

All the information you need to answer the reading questions is given in the passages or in the text of the questions that accompany the passages.

Succeeding on the extended response essay

The Extended Response item is one of the components of the GED test that test-takers worry about the most. Let's face it, not everyone likes to write, and you may even have bad memories of writing essays in school. I can't make all of that go away, but I can give you some strategies and tips that will help you on test day — and in further education, if you decide to go to college.

Remember that a real essay is a work of art that takes days of thinking, research, writing and revision. You can't do all that in 45 minutes, and you don't need to. For a GED essay, you just need to produce a writing sample that demonstrates the critical thinking and writing skills the GED folks are looking for. Understanding the tips in this section will help you do just that!

TIP

A good plan of action is to spend 5 minutes reading and annotating, 10 minutes planning, 20 minutes writing, and 10 minutes editing and revising. This schedule is a tight one, though, so if your keyboarding is slow, consider allowing more time for writing. And remember, no one but you will see anything but the final version, so don't worry if you make mistakes while you type. Keep moving and correct these mistakes when you edit and revise. The following sections explain how to fit each step of this process into the 45 minutes you have to write your essay.

Reading and annotating the prompt (5 minutes)

The essay test has only one item: a prompt on which you have to write a short essay.

The test presents you with two passages of argumentation. That means each writer takes a position on an issue. You must examine the positions, determine which is the stronger and best-defended one, and write an essay of four or more paragraphs explaining why you made that choice. You have to do that regardless of how you feel about the issue. The point is to analyze and show that you understand the strategies used to defend these positions.

Although you cannot choose the topic of your essay, keep in mind that the test developers look for topics that most adults will know something about and be able to relate to. The topics will avoid areas that are sensitive or controversial. You can be sure that politics, religion, and other areas of personal belief will not come up.

Before you begin writing your essay, read the topic carefully (at least twice) and ask yourself what the topic means to you. Determine what the two positions presented in the source texts are.

Next, gather ideas. On the reading screen, you can highlight key pieces of evidence that you want to use in your essay. As you read and highlight, write notes on the erasable tablet or type them into the on-screen whiteboard. In your notes, analyze the arguments for logical consistency, illogical conclusions, and false reasoning. This is where your critical thinking skills come into play. Does Point A from the author really make sense? Is it valid and backed by facts? Don't worry about the order in which you write your ideas, You can sort through all the information in the next phase. Don't worry about correct grammar or spelling either. No one but you will see your notes.

For example, if the essay item presents you with two source texts, one in favor of daylight savings time and the other opposed, and then asks you to evaluate the arguments, you need to begin by considering which text is more convincing — that is, which text presents the better and stronger argument. Then you need to look at and evaluate all the supporting evidence presented by the two sides of the argument.

Planning your essay (10 minutes)

In the planning stage of your essay, look over your highlights and notes and organize them into a logical argument. These steps can guide your planning process:

1. Find an introduction, such as, "The argument that daylight savings time has outlived its usefulness makes the stronger case." Write this sentence above your brainstorming notes.

2. Look at the points you came up with earlier that strongly back up your position. Number them in the most effective order.

3. Add some ideas from the reading that you think are false or flawed, so you can address them in your essay too. All these ideas will be the body of your essay.

REMEMBER

It's important to stick with the points presented in the source texts and not wander off into your own opinions about the topic.

4. Now, write a concluding sentence, such as, "The argument against daylight savings time is stronger. Although once useful, the enormous cost, confusion, and lack of clear benefits show that it's an idea past its time." Glancing at your introduction and the essay topic itself, select points that strengthen your conclusion. Some of these points may be the same ones you used in your introduction.

Your plan will likely look something like this.:

>> **Introduction.** "The argument that daylight savings time has outlived its usefulness makes the stronger case."

>> **Body.**

- List the appropriate supporting evidence in order of importance.
- List false arguments or flawed arguments made by either side of the discussion.

>> **Conclusion.** "Although daylight savings time was helpful in a bygone day, the changeover twice a year costs Americans billions of dollars in needless expense, lost wages, and inconvenience without any clear benefit to people's lives."

Now reflect again. Can you add any more points to improve the essay? Don't just add points to have more points, though. This isn't a contest for who can come up with the most points. You want to have logically written points that support your argument.

Look over your outline again. Can you combine any parts to make it tighter? Do you want to add an example? Or change the organization? Now's the time!

When you are satisfied with your outline, you're ready to go on to the next step: drafting your essay.

Writing (20 minutes)

During the writing stage, you think in more detail about the points you came up with in the planning stage, and type your words on-screen. Begin writing and keep going. Don't get bogged down on spelling or grammar. You can fix those later. Just write organized paragraphs and logical sentences.

REMEMBER

Each paragraph starts with an *introductory sentence*, which sets up the paragraph content, and ends with a *transition sentence* that leads from the paragraph you're on to the next one. If you put your sentences in a logical order from introduction to transition, you start to see paragraphs — as well as your essay — emerge.

Editing and revising (10 minutes)

Now comes the hard part. You have to be your own editor. Turn off your ego and remember that every word is written on a computer screen, not carved in stone. Make your work better by editing and revising it. Make this the best piece of writing you've ever done — in a 45-minute time block, of course.

When you're ready to edit and revise, scroll through your essay twice: once for content and again for standards of conventional English. First, read it to make sure that you are satisfied with the content of the essay. Does it make sense? Does it use good examples from the passages? Does it follow a logical order? If it doesn't, you may need to revise. Ask yourself whether each paragraph contributes to your argument. If it doesn't, you may need to do more revising. It could be something as simple as changing the order of the paragraphs, deleting something, or adding transitional phrases.

Then reread your essay for standards of conventional English. Look for errors in spelling, capitalization, subject-verb agreement, and punctuation. If you quote directly from one of the articles, make sure that you use quotation marks correctly. Check for these errors last because this area is the least important of the criteria used to score your essay. If your essay has good ideas, is written in sentences and paragraphs, flows logically, and has only a few small errors that do not interfere with understanding, you are 90 percent there!

Checking for a winning essay

The key points in the essay evaluation appear in the following list. If you have all these characteristics in your essay, your chances of receiving a high score are pretty good:

>> You've read and understood the two source texts and selected the argument that has the best support.

>> Your essay clearly explains why you made your choice, using proof from the source texts.

>> Your essay is clearly written and well organized.

>> The evidence you present is developed logically and clearly.

>> You use transitions throughout the essay for a smooth flow among ideas.

>> You use appropriate vocabulary, varied sentence structure, and standard English grammar and spelling.

Improving your essay-writing skills

The Extended Response essay requires some very specific skills, ranging from grammar and proper language usage to comprehension and analysis skills. If you've ever had an argument about who has the best team or which employer is better, you already know how to assess arguments and respond. Now you need to hone those skills. As you prepare for the RLA Extended Response, do the following:

TIP

>> **Read, read, and read some more.** Just as for the other parts of the RLA test (and most other tests on the GED), reading is important. Reading exposes you to well-crafted sentences, which can help you improve your own writing.

As you read, make an outline of the paragraphs or chapters that you read to see how the material ties together. Try using your outline to write some of the paragraphs in your own words, and compare what you write to the original. This exercise gives you practice in writing organized, cohesive sentences and paragraphs, which can go a long way on the essay test.

>> **Practice writing on a topic (and not going off topic!).** Your essay must relate to the given topic as closely as possible. If the test asks you to analyze two positions about daylight savings time and you write about how much you love the summertime, you can kiss your good score on this part of the test goodbye.

TIP

To help you practice staying on topic, read the newspaper and write a letter to the editor or a response to a columnist. Because you're responding to a very narrow topic that appeared in a particular newspaper article, you have to do so clearly and concisely — if you ever want to see it in print. You can also find an example essay question in Block 3 and a practice essay in Block 4.

» **Think about and use appropriate examples.** You're dealing with information presented in the source text. You'll find information in the source text that will support or contradict the position you are to argue. When you take a position, you need to use materials from the source text to support your position. Use that information. Look for flaws in the logic. You can find good examples of such arguments in the editorial section of a newspaper or in blogs. Look at how the writers develop their arguments, use logic to support their positions, and perhaps use false logic or flawed reasoning to persuade the readers.

» **Practice editing your own work.** When you take the test, the only person able to edit your essay is you. If that thought scares you, practice editing your own work now. Take a writing workshop or get help from someone who knows how to edit. Practice writing a lot of essays and don't forget to review and edit them as soon as you're done writing.

» **Practice general writing.** If writing connected paragraphs isn't one of your strengths, practice doing so! Write long emails. Write long letters. Write to your member of Congress. Write to your friends. Write articles for community newspapers. Write short stories. Write anything you want — whatever you do, just keep writing.

» **Practice keyboarding.** To write an essay in 45 minutes, you need to be ready to type quickly and accurately. So use a computer as much as possible. To simulate real testing conditions, turn off the spell-checker and grammar-checker. When you finish, turn them back on to get some instant feedback about your work. If you don't own a computer, try to find one at your public library or an adult education center. If the center has classes or tutorials on keyboarding, take advantage of them!

Tackling grammar and language questions

In the Grammar and Language section of the GED, your task is to read, revise, and edit documents that may include how-to information, informational texts, and workplace materials. Because all the questions use the drop-down menu format, you don't have to come up with the answers all on your own. You just have to find each answer among the four choices.

The Grammar and Language component of the RLA test evaluates you on the following types of skills. Note that unlike the other GED test sections, this component of the RLA test expects that you *know* or at least *are familiar with* the rules of grammar. Just looking at the passages provided won't do you much good if you don't understand the basics of these rules already.

» **Mechanics:** You don't have to become a professional writer to pass this test, but you should know or review basic mechanics. Check out *English Grammar For Dummies*, 2nd Edition, by Geraldine Woods (Wiley), or search for specific topics on websites like Grammar Girl (www. quickanddirtytips.com/grammar-girl/) or Khan Academy (www.khanacademy.org) to review what you should know or may have forgotten. The mechanics of writing include the following:

- **Capitalization:** You have to recognize which words start with a capital letter and which words don't. All sentences start with a capital letter, but so do titles, like *Miss, President,* and *Senator,* when they're followed by a person's name. Names of cities, states, and countries are also capitalized.

- **Punctuation:** This area of writing mechanics includes everyone's personal favorite: commas. (Actually, most people hate commas because they aren't sure how to use them, but the basic rules are simple.) The more you read, the better you get at punctuation. If you're reading and don't understand why punctuation is or isn't used, check with your grammar guidebook or the Internet.

The comma is the most misused punctuation mark in English. Always think carefully before you add or remove a comma.

- **Spelling:** You don't have to spot a lot of misspelled words, but you do have to know how to spell contractions and possessives and understand the different spellings of *homonyms* — words that sound the same but have different spellings and meanings, like *their* and *there.*

- **Contractions:** This area of writing mechanics has nothing to do with those painful moments before childbirth! Instead, *contractions* are formed when the English language shortens and combines two words by leaving out one or more letters. For example, when you say or write *can't,* you're using a shortened form of *cannot.*

The important thing to remember about contractions is that the *apostrophe* (that's a single quotation mark) takes the place of the letter or letters that are left out. That's why we write *can't.* The apostrophe takes the place of *n* and *o.*

- **Possessives:** Do you know people who are possessive? They're all about ownership, right? So is the grammar form of possessives. *Possessives* are words that show ownership or possession, usually by adding an apostrophe and an *s* to a person's or object's name. If Marcia owns a car, that car is *Marcia's* car. The word *Marcia's* is a possessive. Make sure you know the difference between singular and plural possessives. For example: "The girl**'s** coat is torn." *(Girl* is singular, so the apostrophe goes before the *s.)* "The girls**'** coats are torn." *(Girls* is plural, so the apostrophe goes after the *s.)* When working with plural possessives, form the plural first and then add the apostrophe.

Some plural nouns, such as *women,* do not end in *s,* so the plural possessive is formed with *'s:* "The women**'s** coats are torn."

- ❯❯ **Grammar:** Grammar focuses on the basic rules for forming correct sentences. As with mechanics, *English Grammar For Dummies,* Grammar Girl, or Khan Academy can help you with commonly tested items such as the following.

  - **Complete and incomplete sentences:** These include run-on sentences, sentence fragments, and improperly joined sentences. For example, "The quick red fox jumped over the lazy brown dog the dog kept on sleeping," runs two sentences together. Fix the error with a comma and *but:* "The quick red fox jumped over the lazy brown dog, **but** the dog kept on sleeping."

  - **Proper agreement:** In written English, the subject and the verb of a sentence should agree. For example, "Matilda and her sister is watching TV and knitting" is incorrect. To correct this sentence, change *is* to *are* to agree with the subject of the sentence, *Matilda and her sister,* which is plural.

  - **Correct word order:** Words should be in the correct order. For example, "She bought some orange, ugly, fake flowers," should be changed to, "She bought some ugly, fake, orange flowers."

Extensive reading before the test can give you a good idea of how good sentences are structured and put together. The advice here is to read, read, and read some more.

- ❯❯ **Usage:** This broad category covers a lot of topics. English has a wide variety of rules, and these questions test your knowledge and understanding of those rules. Verbs have tenses that must be consistent. Pronouns must refer back to nouns properly. If the last two sentences sound like Greek to you, make sure you review usage rules. They also cover vocabulary and standard English usage. People have become very comfortable with short forms used in texting, but "LOL" or "C U L8R" aren't acceptable in standard writing.

Having a firm grasp of these writing conventions can help you get a more accurate picture of the types of questions you'll encounter on this part of the test.

Surveying the Social Studies Test

The GED Social Studies test assesses your skills in understanding and interpreting concepts and principles in civics, history, geography, and economics. Consider this test as a kind of crash course in where you've been, where you are, and how you can continue living there. You can apply the types of skills tested on the Social Studies test to your experience in community, school, and workplace situations as a citizen, a consumer, or an employee.

This test includes questions based on a variety of written passages and visual content taken from academic, community, and workplace materials, including both primary and secondary sources. The materials in this test are like those you see in most online news content. Reading well-written, reliable news sources regularly can help you become familiar with the style and vocabulary of the passages you find on the GED. Pay attention to articles on politics, the government, the Supreme Court, and the economy. For history, any number of websites have articles on U.S. or world history.

The Social Studies test consists of 50 multiple-choice questions on civics and government (about 50 percent of the test), U.S. history (about 20 percent of the test), economics (about 15 percent of the test), and geography and the world (about 15 percent of the test). You have 70 minutes to complete this section.

The types of questions that you encounter on the Social Studies test include multiple-choice, fill-in-the-blank, drag-and-drop, and drop-down-menu.

There are two broad categories of source materials for the questions on the test. These source materials consist of textual materials, something with which you're probably already quite familiar, and visuals like maps, diagrams, graphs, and tables. Each kind of material requires careful reading, even the visuals, because information can be buried anywhere, and you need to extract it. The materials require you to read thoughtfully, make inferences, come to conclusions, and then determine the answer. The following sections help you understand the questions that use these different materials.

Questions about text passages

About half of the questions on the Social Studies test are based on textual passages, followed by a question or a series of questions. Your job is to read the passage and then answer the question or questions about it.

When you're reading these passages on the test (or in any of the practice questions or tests in this book), read between the lines and look at the implications and assumptions in the passages. An *implication* is something you can understand from what's written, even though it isn't directly stated. An *assumption* is something you can accept as the truth, even though proof isn't directly presented in the text.

REMEMBER

Be sure to read each question carefully so you know exactly what it's asking. Read the answer choices and go through the text again, carefully. If the question asks for certain facts, you'll be able to find them right in the passage. If it asks for opinions, you may find those opinions stated directly in the passage, or they may simply be implied (and they may not match your own opinions, but you still have to answer with the best choice based on the material presented).

Answer each question using *only* the information given. An answer may be incorrect in your opinion, but according to the passage, it's correct (or vice versa). Go with the information presented and select the best answer choice.

Questions about visual materials

To make sure you don't get bored, many of the questions on the Social Studies test are based on maps, graphs, tables, political cartoons, diagrams, photographs, and artistic works. You need to be prepared to deal with all these types of visual materials. Some questions combine visual material and text.

TIP

If you're unsure of how to read a map, go to any search engine and search for "map reading help" or "map reading skills" to find sites that explain how to read a map. If any of the other types of visual materials cause you concern, try similar searches, such as "graph reading skills," "understanding tables," or "interpreting political cartoons." You will get lots of tips and advice, plus plenty of maps, graphs, tables, and political cartoons to look at.

All the visual items you have to review on this test should be familiar to you. Now all you have to do is practice until your skills in reading and understanding them increase. Then you, too, can discuss the latest political cartoon or pontificate about a work of art. The following sections offer tips on interpreting each type of visual material you might see on the GED.

Maps

Maps show you more than the location of places. They also give you information, and knowing how to decode that information is essential. A map may show you where Charleston is located, but it can also show you how the land around Charleston is used, what the climate in the area is like, or whether the population there is growing or declining. Start by examining the print information with the map, the *legend* (the table explaining the symbols used on the map), title, and key to the colors or symbols on the map. Then look at what the question requires you to find. Now you can find that information quickly by relating the answer choices to what the map shows.

For example, the map in Figure 2-1 shows you the following information:

>> The population of the United States for 2020

>> The population by state, by size range

Indirectly, the map also shows you much more. It allows you to compare the population of states with a quick glance. For example, you can see that Florida has a larger population than Montana, North Dakota, South Dakota, and Wyoming combined. If you were asked what the relationship is between a state's size and population, you could argue, based on this map, that there isn't much relationship. You could also show that the states in the northeast have a higher population density than the states in the Midwest. This is part of the skill of analyzing maps.

Graphs

Every time you turn around, someone in the media is trying to make a point with a graph. The types of graphs you see in Figure 2-2 are very typical examples. The real reason people use graphs to explain themselves so often is that a graph can clearly show trends and relationships between different sets of information. The three graphs in Figure 2-2 are best suited for a particular use. For example, bar graphs are great for comparing items over time, line graphs show changes over time, and pie charts show you proportions. The next time you see a graph, such as the ones in Figure 2-2, study it.

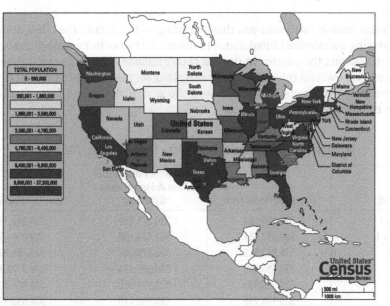

FIGURE 2-1: Population of U.S. states, District of Columbia, and Puerto Rico, 2020 Census Map.

Source: Adapted from U.S. Census Bureau

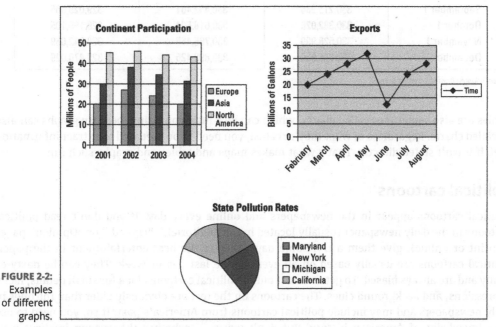

FIGURE 2-2: Examples of different graphs.

© John Wiley & Sons, Inc.

Be sure to look carefully at the scale of graphs; even visual information can fool you. A bar graph that appears to show a rapid rise of something may, in fact, show no such thing. It may only look that way because the bottom of the chart doesn't start with values of zero. Check carefully to make sure you understand what the information in the graph is telling you.

Tables

Tables are everywhere. If you've ever looked at the nutrition label on a food product, you've read a table. Study any table you can find, whether in a newspaper or on the back of a can of tuna. The population data table in Figure 2-3 is an example of the kinds of data you may see on the test. That table shows you a lot of information, but you can extract quite a bit more information that isn't stated. Some mental math tells you that according to the data in the table, around 236,000 people were serving outside the United States in the armed forces in December 2020. How do you know that? Just subtract the number in the *Resident Population* column from the *Resident Population Plus Armed Forces Overseas* column. You can also calculate the change in the overall population, the rate of increase of the population, and even the size of the armed forces stationed in the United States compared to serving overseas.

Monthly Population Estimates for the United States, 2020

Month	Resident Population	Resident Population Plus Armed Forces Overseas	Civilian Population
January 1	329,135,084	329,371,559	327,948,163
February 1	329,237,661	329,474,136	328,050,740
March 1	329,342,883	329,579,358	328,155,962
April 1	329,459,499	329,695,974	328,272,578
May 1	329,588,430	329,824,905	328,401,509
June 1	329,726,295	329,962,770	328,539,374
July 1	329,877,505	330,113,980	328,690,584
August 1	330,047,526	330,284,001	328,860,605
September 1	330,215,986	330,452,461	329,029,065
October 1	330,382,026	330,618,501	329,195,105
November 1	330,528,990	330,765,465	329,342,069
December 1	330,656,950	330,893,425	329,470,029

FIGURE 2-3: Population data table.

Source: Adapted from U.S. Census Bureau

REMEMBER

Tables are also sometimes called charts, which can be a little confusing, because graphs can also be called charts. Regardless of what they're called, you need to be prepared to extract information even if it isn't stated directly. That's what makes maps and tables and graphs such fun.

Political cartoons

Political cartoons appear in the newspapers and online every day. If you don't read political cartoons in the daily newspaper (usually located in the "Editorial," "Op-Ed," or "Opinion" pages in print or online), give them a try. Some days, they're the best entertainment in the paper. Political cartoons are usually based on an event in the last day or week. They can be nasty or funny and are always biased. To get the most out of political cartoons, look for small details, facial expressions, and background clues. The cartoons on the test are obviously older than the ones in daily newspapers and may include political cartoons from America's past. If so, you need to use your knowledge of American history. But don't worry — whether the cartoon is about war, politics, or the economy, the context will be clear. To become more familiar with past cartoons, search for "political cartoons" online. You can also find websites that build skills for interpreting political cartoons.

Photographs and artwork

You've no doubt seen countless photographs in your day. Photos are all around you. All you need to do to prepare for the photograph-based questions on the test is to begin getting information from the photographs you see. Start with the newspapers or magazines, where photos are chosen to provide information that connects directly to a story. See whether you can determine what message the photograph carries with it and how it relates to the story it supports. Use the caption to help you understand the photo. If you don't understand a word or two in the caption, use information from the photo to help you figure it out.

You probably like to look at works of art. On the Social Studies test, you have a chance to "read" works of art. You look at a work of art and gather information you can use to answer the item. To get yourself ready to gather information from works of art on the test, visit an art museum (in person or online), go on the Internet, or check out some library books. Luckily for you, books and websites even give background and other explanations for these works. Online, the Smithsonian National Museum of American History (https://americanhistory.si.edu) is a good place to start.

Peering into the Science Test

Did you know that the passing rate for the GED Science test is 90 percent? That's because the GED Science test doesn't test you on the depth of your knowledge of science. You're not expected to memorize any scientific information to do well on this test. Instead, this test assesses your ability to ferret out information presented in passages or visual materials. However, you should have at least a passing background knowledge of science and scientific vocabulary. I explain the topics you're asked to read and answer questions about later in this section.

TIP

One of the best ways to improve your understanding of science material and scientific vocabulary is to read scientific material, science magazines, websites, and even old textbooks. Look up any words you don't know. Rest easy that you aren't expected to know the scientific difference between terms like *fission* and *fusion* — but just being familiar with them can help you on the test.

And there's more good news! Since the Science test is based on your ability to read and interpret textual material, your preparation for the Reading Comprehension section of the Reading and Language Arts test will help you on the Science test — and vice versa!

The Science test covers material from life science, physical science (chemistry and physics), and earth and space science. You're asked to read and understand the material and answer questions correctly.

As you prepare to take the Science test, you're expected to understand that science is all about inquiry. In fact, inquiry forms the basis of the *scientific method* — the process every good scientist follows when faced with an unknown. The steps of the scientific method are as follows:

1. **Ask questions.**
2. **Gather information.**
3. **Do experiments.**
4. **Think objectively about what you find.**
5. **Look at other possible explanations.**
6. **Draw one or more possible conclusions.**
7. **Test the conclusion(s).**
8. **Tell others what you found.**

FINDING SCIENCE ON THE INTERNET

The Internet can increase your scientific knowledge or simply introduce you to a new area of interest. If you don't have an Internet connection at home or through a cell phone, try your local library or community center.

To save yourself time as you begin your online search for additional practice in reading science material, I suggest that you check out the following sites:

- `www.els.net`: Contains tons of information about life sciences.

- `https://solarsystem.nasa.gov`: Contains lots of intriguing earth- and space-related information.

- `www.thoughtco.com/chemistry-4133594`: Contains interesting information related to chemistry. (Note that this is a commercial site, which means you'll see pesky banners and commercial links amidst the interesting and helpful information.)

- `www.thoughtco.com/physics-4133571`: Contains some interesting physics lessons that are presented in an entertaining and informative manner.

- `https://ged.com`: The GED Testing Service's site, which contains a great deal of information, both general and specific, regarding the Science test.

To explore on your own, go to your favorite search engine and type the science keywords you're most interested in (*biology, earth science,* and *chemistry,* just to name a few examples). You can also use the same keywords for a YouTube search and find many excellent videos explaining these topics.

Understanding the test format and topics

The Science test contains about 50 questions of different formats, which you have 90 minutes to answer. As with the other test sections, the information and questions on the Science test are straightforward — no one is trying to trick you. To answer the questions, you have to read and interpret the passages or other visual materials provided with the questions (and you need a basic understanding of science and the words scientists use when they communicate).

In terms of organization, some of the items are grouped in sets. Some items are stand-alone questions based on one issue or topic. Some questions follow a given passage, chart, diagram, graph, map, or table. Your job is to read or review the material and decide on the best answer for each question based on the given material.

In terms of subject matter, the questions on the Science test check your knowledge in the following areas.

>> **Physical science:** About 40 percent of the test is about *physical science,* which is the study of atoms, chemical reactions, forces, and what happens when energy and matter get together. As a basic review, keep the following in mind:

- Everything is composed of atoms, even the paper or computer screen you're reading right now!

- When chemicals get together, they have a reaction — unless they're *inert* (which means they don't react with other chemicals; inert chemicals are sort of like antisocial chemicals).

- You're surrounded by forces and their effects. (If the floor didn't exert a force up on you when you stepped down, you would go through the floor.)

>> **Life science:** Another 40 percent of the test covers *life science* — the study of cells, heredity, and other processes that occur in living systems. All life is composed of *cells,* which you can see under a microscope. Most life science–related books and websites have photographs of cells that you can study. When someone tells you that you look like your parents or that you remind them of another relative, they're talking about *heredity.* Reading a bit about heredity in biology-related books can help you practice answering some of the questions on the Science test.

>> **Earth and space science:** The remaining 20 percent of the test covers earth and space science. This area of science looks at the earth and the universe, specifically weather, astronomy, geology, rocks, erosion, and water.

   When you look down at the ground as you walk, you're interacting with earth science. When you look up at the stars on a clear night and wonder what's really up there, you're thinking about space science. When you complain about the weather, you're complaining about earth science. In a nutshell, you're surrounded by earth and space sciences, so you shouldn't have a problem finding materials to read on this subject.

The topics on the Science test are focused on two main themes, both of which you probably deal with on some level every day.

>> **Human health and living systems:** Who isn't concerned with being safe and healthy? After all, it's your body and you need it. Most people try to eat nutritious meals, get some exercise, and avoid getting sick. Understanding the human body and other living organisms is an important part of science knowledge.

>> **Energy and related systems:** Energy powers your cars, cooks your food, heats your home, turns on your lights, and keeps the planet going. Understanding how energy flows through organisms and ecosystems can help you navigate your daily life and succeed on the Science test.

REMEMBER

You don't have to memorize everything you read about science before you take the test. All the answers to the test questions are based on information provided in the passages, or on the basic knowledge about science that you've acquired over the years. However, any science reading you do before the test increases your basic knowledge and improves your vocabulary. An improved science vocabulary increases your chances of understanding and analyzing the passages and answering the related test questions quickly.

Analyzing scientific text passages

The text passages on this test — and the questions that accompany them — are very similar to a reading-comprehension test: You're given textual material and you have to answer questions about it. The passages present everything you need to answer the questions, but you usually have to understand all the words used in those passages to figure out what they're telling you (which is why I recommend that you read as much science information as you can prior to the test).

The difference between the text passages on the Science test and other reading-comprehension tests is that the terminology and examples are all about science. Thus, the more you read about science, the more science words you'll know, understand, and be comfortable seeing on the test — which, as you may imagine, can greatly improve your chances of success.

Keep the following tips and tricks in mind when answering questions about text passages:

» **Read each passage and question carefully.** Some of the questions on the Science test assume that you know a little bit from past experience. For example, you may be expected to know that a rocket is propelled forward by an engine firing backward. As you read, do the following:

  • Try to understand the passage and think about what you already know about the subject.

  • If a passage has only one question, read that question extra carefully.

  • If the passage or question contains words you don't understand, try to figure out what those words mean from the rest of the sentence, the entire passage, or any graphic or illustration. However, if you still understand the overall main idea without knowing that word, you can skip the word and go on.

» **Read each answer choice carefully.** Doing so helps you get a clearer picture of your options and eliminate obviously wrong answers, as explained in Block 1. Then you can look more closely at the choices that might be correct and identify choices that are only partially correct. Another answer choice may be more complete or accurate. If you cannot answer a question, remember that you can use the flag feature to mark the question and return to it later if you have more time.

Interpreting graphs, tables, and other visual materials

The types of visual materials you see on the Science test are similar to those on the Social Studies test: tables, graphs, diagrams, photos, and maps. (You can see examples of these visual materials earlier in this block.) On the Science test, these visual materials simply focus on Science content, such as lab test results.

Any visual object is like a short paragraph. It has a topic and makes comments or states facts about that topic. When you come across a question based on visual material, the first thing to do is to figure out the content or topic of the material. Usually, visual objects have titles or captions that help you understand their meanings, so read those first. If you don't understand any of the words, use the image to help you figure out the words. After you understand the main idea behind the visual object, ask yourself what information you're being given and what information you need to find out; reading the question can be helpful. After you know these two pieces of information, you're well on your way to answering the question.

The following sections take a more detailed look at the different visual materials that you may find on the Science test.

Tables

A *table* is a graphical way of organizing information. This type of visual material allows for easy comparison between two or more sets of data. Some tables use numbers and symbols to represent information; others use words.

Most tables have titles that tell you what they're about. Always read the titles first so you know right away what information the tables include. If a table gives you an explanation (or *key*) of the symbols, read the explanation carefully, too; doing so helps you understand how to read the table.

Graphs

A *graph* is a picture that shows how different sets of numbers are related. On the Science test, you can find the following three main types of graphs.

>> **Bar or column graphs:** Bar (horizontal) or column (vertical) graphs present and often compare numbers or quantities.

>> **Line graphs:** On line graphs, one or more lines connect points drawn on a grid to show the relationships between data, including changes in data over time.

>> **Pie graphs (also called pie charts or circle graphs):** Arcs of circles (pieces of a pie) show how data relates to a whole. Often, data in pie charts is expressed as a percent of a whole.

All three types of graphs usually share the following common characteristics.

>> **Title:** The title tells you what the graph is about, so always read the title before reviewing the graph.

>> **Horizontal axis and vertical axis:** Bar, column, and line graphs have a horizontal axis and a vertical axis. (Pie graphs don't.) Each axis is a vertical or horizontal reference line that's labeled to give you additional information.

>> **Label:** The labels on the axes of a graph usually contain units, such as feet or dollars. Read all axis labels carefully; they can either help you with the answer or lead you astray (depending on whether you read them correctly). The labels in a pie chart will indicate the unit of measurement and the quantities (often percent).

>> **Legend:** Graphs usually have a *legend,* or printed material that tells you what each section of the graph is about. They may also contain labels on the individual parts of the graph and explanatory notes about the data used to create the graph, so read carefully.

WARNING

Graphs and tables are both often called *charts*, which can be rather confusing. To help you prepare for problems with graphs, make sure you look at and understand plenty of graphs before the test. Remember that graphs show relationships. If the numbers represented on the horizontal axis are in millions of dollars and you think they're in dollars, your interpretation of the graph will be more than a little incorrect.

Diagrams

A *diagram* is a drawing that helps you understand how something works. Diagrams on the Science test often have the following two components.

>> **Title:** Tells you what the diagram is trying to show you.

>> **Labels:** Indicate the names of the parts of the diagram.

When you come to a question based on a diagram, read the title of the diagram first to get an idea of what the diagram is about. Then carefully read all the labels to find out the main components of the diagram. These two pieces of information can help you understand the diagram well enough to answer questions about it.

Photos

A *photo* may sometimes appear on the GED. You can use these features of photos to help you understand them.

>> **Caption:** The caption tells you the subject of the photo. For example, a photo of the planet Mars may identify the planet and say how the photo was taken: "A space probe took this close-up photo of the planet Mars."

>> **Labels:** Labels may mark or identify people or objects in the photo. For example, a photo of Mars may have its ice cap labeled.

When you come to a question based on a photo, read the caption first. Then carefully read any labels. Then look at the photo. If you don't understand any words in the label, use the photo to figure them out.

Maps

A *map* is a drawing of some section — large or small — of the earth or another planet. People even call images of the solar system or of the stars in the night sky a map. Because the entire world is too large to depict on one piece of paper, maps are drawn to scale.

Most maps give you the following information.

>> **Title:** Tells you what area of the world the map focuses on and what it shows.

>> **Legend:** Gives you general information about the meaning, colors, symbols, or other graphics used on the map.

>> **Compass:** Indicates the map's orientation. In general, north is at the top of a map, but for certain maps, this may not be the case. On many maps, a small compass will show which way is north. (Sometimes this compass may be omitted if the map is very familiar. A map of the United States likely would not have a compass, as most people know the north is at the top.)

>> **Labels:** Indicate what the various points on the map represent.

>> **Scale:** Tells you what the distance on the map represents in real life. (For example, a map with a scale of 1 inch = 100 miles shows a distance of 500 miles on the real earth as a distance of 5 inches on the map.)

Although maps are seldom used in science passages, they are used occasionally, so you want to be familiar with them. And you will certainly encounter them on the Social Studies test. The best way to get familiar with maps is to spend some time looking at road maps and world atlases, which you can find in your local library or online.

REMEMBER

The exact meaning of any visual materials may not be obvious or may even be misleading if not examined carefully. You must understand what the legends, scale, labels, and color-coding are telling you. Numbers on a table also may be misleading or even meaningless unless you read the legend and labels carefully. Colors on a map aren't just for decoration; each color has a meaning. Each piece of a visual represents meaning from which you can put together the information you need to determine the answers to test questions.

Sizing Up the Math Test

The Mathematical Reasoning test is different from other GED tests. It tests your understanding of mathematical concepts and your ability to apply them to situations you may find in the real world. That means that you have to spend time solving as many problems as you can and improving your math skills as much as possible before you take this test. But it also means you've been using some of this math in your day-to-day life, perhaps without even realizing it! For example, when you figure out how much time you need to get someplace or calculate your savings with a coupon or discount, you are using the same math you see on the GED.

This section helps you prepare for the GED math test by introducing the test format and the skills it covers and then providing some tips and tricks for tackling the test. After you review this section, check out the sample questions in Block 3 and the practice test questions in Block 4. After you identify what you math you know and what you need to review, you can use a website like Khan Academy (www.khanacademy.org) to learn or review math skills you need for the GED.

The Mathematical Reasoning test is 115 minutes long and consists of multiple-choice, drop-down, drag-and-drop, and fill-in-the-blank questions, but it doesn't have any type of essay question. You really have to be thankful for small mercies!

Identifying the math skills you need

To do well on the Math test, you need to have a general understanding of numbers, their relationships to one another, measurements, geometry, data analysis and statistics, probability, patterns, functions, and algebra. In essence, to be successful on this test, you need to have the mathematical knowledge base that most high-school graduates have, and you need to know how to apply it to solve real-life problems.

REMEMBER

The GED Math test provides a formula sheet for you to use during the test. Keep in mind that you may not need all the formulas provided, and you will not need a formula for every question. Part of the fun of math is knowing which formula to use for which problems and figuring out when you don't need one at all. You may want to memorize some of the more common formulas to save time. But when you need a formula, you can look it up. You don't have to memorize them all! That makes preparing easier.

The Math test assesses the following four areas.

>> **Basic math:** This area of math covers, you guessed it, the basics! Here's a breakdown of the two topics in this category:

  ● *Number operations* are the familiar actions you take in math problems and equations, such as addition, subtraction, multiplication, and division. You probably mastered these operations in grade school; now all you have to do is practice them.

  ● *Number sense* is the ability to understand numbers. You're expected to be able to recognize different kinds of numbers (such as fractions, decimals, percentages, and square roots), know their relative values, and know how to use them (which takes us back to number operations).

TIP

About half of the Math test depends on basic arithmetic (addition, subtraction, multiplication, division, decimals, and fractions). The better you know the fundamentals, the better you can do on the test.

>> **Geometry:** Here, you get a chance to play with mathematical shapes and manipulate them in your head — and on the GED's on-screen whiteboard. You get to use the Pythagorean Theorem to do all sorts of interesting calculations, and you get to use measurements to do things like find the volume of ice cream in a cone or the amount of wall you need to cover with paint. If you prepare using the sample questions in Block 3 and the shortened practice test in Block 4, you can have fun with these questions and then maybe even use a lot of the knowledge in real life. This category breaks down into two topics:

- *Measurement* involves area, volume, time, and the distance from here to there. Measurement of time is a good thing to know when taking any test because you want to make sure that you run out of questions before you run out of time!

- *Geometry* deals with relationships and properties of points, lines, angles, and shapes (such as squares, circles, and triangles). This branch of math requires you to draw, use, and understand diagrams.

>> **Basic algebra:** Algebra is used to solve problems by using *variables* (which are letters that represent unknown numbers), creating equations from the information given, and solving for the unknown numbers — thus, turning them into known numbers. If you ever said something like, "How much more does the $10 scarf cost than the $7.50 one?" you were really solving this equation: $\$7.50 + x = \$10.00$.

>> **Graphs and functions:** Graphs and functions allow you to analyze data. You can learn how to analyze data in graphs, tables, and the coordinate plane.

- *Data analysis* is when you see a graph of the stock market's performance (or lack of performance), calculate or read about baseball statistics, or figure out how many miles per gallon your car gets. See the earlier sections about graphs for help interpreting them.

- *Functions* are part of mathematics. They involve the concept that one number can be determined by its relationship with another. A dozen always consists of 12 units, for example. If you were buying two dozen eggs, you'd be buying $12 \times 2 = 24$ eggs.

- *The coordinate plane* graphically shows the location of points on the plane or a line and helps you to determine such things as the slope, or steepness, of a line.

Using a calculator, formula sheets, and special symbols

During the Mathematical Reasoning test, you can use the on-screen (or your own) TI-30XS MultiView calculator for all but the first five questions. Before you start celebrating, remember that the calculator is an instrument that makes calculations easier. It doesn't solve problems or perform other miracles. You still have to solve the problems using the computer between your ears.

The test also has a formula sheet. This feature also isn't a miracle that can work out problems for you. It's just a memory aid if you don't remember the formulas. And as a special treat, the Math test also provides symbols for you to use in the fill-in-the-blank items as needed. I explore all these features in the following sections. You can find a tutorial on these special features on the GED website, at https://app.ged.com/portal/tips. Log in and select "Get to Know the Test."

REMEMBER

One of the most valuable tools for preparing for the GED is an account at ged.com. Besides being the place where you sign up to take the test, this website offers tools and study aids. You have to be logged into your account to access many of the special features I reference in this section.

Solving questions with and without a calculator

For all but the first five items in the Math test, you can use a calculator. You have to finish the first five items before you go on to questions that use the calculator. To pull up the calculator on the computerized GED Math test, click the calculator icon. A calculator — a Texas Instruments TI-30XS MultiView calculator to be exact — appears on-screen. (See Block 1 for an introduction to the calculator.)

It's a good idea to get familiar with the calculator before taking the GED test. You can either use the one on the GED Testing Service website for practice or find an identical hand-held one. (The computer version of the calculator operates just like the hand-held device.) Then make sure you know how to solve the various types of mathematical problems, and only depend on the calculator to do mechanical operations more quickly and easily.

TIP

Often, solving a problem without a calculator is faster than using a calculator, especially with multiple-choice questions where you have four answer choices to choose from. And the more questions you practice in your head, the easier it will be. Here are some ways to practice solving problems in your head (without a calculator):

>> When you go shopping, add up the prices as you put items in your cart. Check your total at the cash register.

>> Calculate discounts off items you see or buy when you shop.

>> Be the first at your table in a restaurant to figure out the tip. And for bonus practice, figure out different tip percentages on your bill, such as 15, 18, and 20 percent tips.

TIP

For multiple-choice questions, sometimes estimating the answer to a question is easier and faster. For example, 4.2×8.9 is almost 4×9, which equals 36. If only one answer choice is close to 36, that choice is probably correct. If you see that two or more answer choices are close to 36, however, you need to spend time calculating the exact answer.

Refreshing your memory with the formula sheet

The GED Math test includes a formula sheet with a list of formulas that you may need for the test. You simply click on the formula icon to make the page of formulas appear. Unfortunately, no genie will appear to tell you which formula to use. Figuring out which formula you need is your job.

To get familiar with the formulas you may need on the GED test, study the formulas on the example formula sheet in Block 4 and make sure you know their purpose. Then make sure you understand what kind of problem each formula helps you solve. For example, if you have a formula for the volume of a rectangular cube and the question asks you how many cubic feet of water a swimming pool contains, you know this formula will enable you to work out the answer. If the question asks you how many tiles it takes to go around the rim of the pool, you need a different formula.

Inserting special symbols

When answering fill-in-the-blank items, you sometimes need to insert special symbols. These formulas are mainly math symbols, such as add or subtract, greater than or less than, equals, pi (π), and so on. You can see all the symbols at the beginning of the practice test in Block 4.

To make a symbol appear in the fill-in-the-blank box on the test, click the symbols icon at the top of the screen (Æ), and then click the symbol you want to include in the box. You can also use the symbols in the online whiteboard. You can find a tutorial on these special features on the GED website, at `https://app.ged.com/portal/tips`. After you log in, select "Get to Know the Test."

Block 3
Working Through Some Practice Questions

The best way to get ready for the GED tests is to practice. These sample questions help you evaluate your skills in a wide variety of areas. If you have time, you can try all these questions. But this is *GED Test 5-Hour Quick Prep For Dummies,* and I promised this block would take only an hour. So, to get through these questions in an hour or less, focus on answering the ones you don't understand and then use the answers and explanations at the end of each section to identify whether you got the correct answer. If you answered incorrectly, review the concept to improve your understanding. Then you'll be ready for the shortened practice test in Block 4.

Record your answers either directly in this book or on a sheet of paper, if you think you might want to try these practice questions again at a later date. *Remember:* This is just preliminary practice. I want you to get used to answering different types of questions.

Reasoning through Language Arts Sample Questions

The official Reasoning through Language Arts test has three sections, and you find sample questions for each in the following sections. If you have time to practice the extended response, I suggest typing your essay so you practice your word-processing skills. Remember that the GED word processor does not have a spelling and grammar checker, so turn it off to remind yourself to watch for typing mistakes on the test.

RLA Reading Comprehension

The Reading component of the RLA test consists of excerpts from nonfiction and fiction prose. Multiple-choice and drag-and-drop questions based on the reading material follow each excerpt.

For the multiple-choice questions in this section, choose the one best answer to each question. For the drag-and-drop items, write the letters of the answers in the boxes. Work carefully, but don't spend too much time on any one question. Be sure to answer every question. You can find the answers for these questions later in this section.

Questions

Questions 1–8 refer to the following article from the United States Geological Service Newsroom (www. usgs.gov).

(1) USGS scientists and Icelandic partners found avian flu viruses from North America and Europe in migratory birds in Iceland, demonstrating that the North Atlantic is as significant as the North Pacific in being a melting pot for birds and avian flu. A great number of wild birds from Europe and North America congregate and mix in Iceland's wetlands during migration, where infected birds could transmit avian flu viruses to healthy birds from either location.

(2) By crossing the Atlantic Ocean this way, avian flu viruses from Europe could eventually be transported to the United States. This commingling could also lead to the evolution of new influenza viruses. These findings are critical for proper surveillance and monitoring of flu viruses, including the H5N1 avian influenza that can infect humans.

(3) "None of the avian flu viruses found in our study are considered harmful to humans," said Robert Dusek, USGS scientist and lead author of the study. "However, the results suggest that Iceland is an important location for the study of avian flu. . . ."

(4) During the spring and autumn of 2010 and autumn of 2011, the USGS researchers and Icelandic partners collected avian influenza viruses from gulls and waterfowl in southwest and west Iceland. . . . By studying the viruses' genomes . . . the researchers found that some viruses came from Eurasia and some originated in North America. They also found viruses with mixed American-Eurasian lineages.

(5) "For the first time, avian influenza viruses from both Eurasia and North America were documented at the same location and time," said Jeffrey Hall, USGS co-author and principal investigator on this study. "Viruses are continually evolving, and this mixing of viral strains sets the stage for new types of avian flu to develop."

1. How dangerous is this new potential source of avian flu to humans?

   (A) very dangerous
   (B) not at all dangerous
   (C) a concern but not particularly dangerous
   (D) serious enough that it requires monitoring

2. Before this discovery, where did scientists believe most birds carrying the avian flu intermingled with North American birds?

   (A) South Pacific
   (B) Central America
   (C) Eurasia
   (D) North Pacific

3. Why was the finding of Eurasian, North American, and mixed virus genomes in the same locale significant?

(A) It proved avian flu viruses comingle only in the North Pacific.

(B) It proved that the avian flu is a risk to humans.

(C) It proved that avian flu viruses had mingled in Iceland.

(D) It proved that Iceland is the origin of the avian flu.

4. Why is the mixing of avian flu viruses in Iceland an important concern?

(A) It can lead to a new, dangerous strain of avian flu.

(B) Cold viruses are constantly evolving.

(C) It provides lead time to develop new vaccines.

(D) It suggests tourists avoid that area.

5. Which of these terms best describes the tone of this passage?

(A) light-hearted

(B) deeply concerned

(C) factual and straightforward

(D) gloomy

6. Which strain of the avian flu virus can infect humans?

(A) the bird flu

(B) the H5N1 strain

(C) the avian H5 flu

(D) the Eurasian avian flu

7. How does the word *however* in Paragraph 3 function in the passage?

(A) It indicates that avian flu is not a risk to humans.

(B) It contrasts the situation in Iceland and the North Pacific.

(C) It indicates the writer's skepticism about the scientists' claims.

(D) It shifts the focus from risk to humans to the need for continued monitoring.

8. Which of these statements is essential to a summary of the article? Which are not essential? Write the letters of the statements in the correct boxes.

Essential to a Summary	Not Essential to a Summary

(A) The scientists studied gulls in southwest Iceland.

(B) Analysis revealed viruses with mixed Asian and American genomes.

(C) None of the viruses found to date are harmful to humans.

(D) The birds congregated in Iceland's wetlands.

Questions 9–16 refer to the following excerpt from Robert Bloch's short story, "This Crowded Earth" (1958).

(1) The telescreen lit up promptly at eight a.m. Smiling Brad came on with his usual greeting. "Good morning — it's a beautiful day in Chicagee!"

(2) Harry Collins rolled over and twitched off the receiver. "This I doubt," he muttered. He sat up and reached into the closet for his clothing. Visitors — particularly feminine ones — were always exclaiming over the advantages of Harry's apartment. "So convenient," they would say. "Everything handy, right within reach. And think of all the extra steps you save!"

(3) Of course most of them were just being polite and trying to cheer Harry up. They knew damned well that he wasn't living in one room through any choice of his own. The Housing Act was something you just couldn't get around; not in Chicagee these days. A bachelor was entitled to one room — no more and no less. And even though Harry was making a speedy buck at the agency, he couldn't hope to beat the regulations.

(4) There was only one way to beat them and that was to get married. Marriage would automatically entitle him to two rooms — *if* he could find them someplace. More than a few of his feminine visitors had hinted at just that, but Harry didn't respond. Marriage was no solution, the way he figured it. He knew that he couldn't hope to locate a two-room apartment any closer than eighty miles away. It was bad enough driving forty miles to and from work every morning and night without doubling the distance. If he did find a bigger place, that would mean a three-hour trip each way on one of the commutrains, and the commutrains were murder. The Black Hole of Calcutta, on wheels. But then, everything was murder, Harry reflected, as he stepped from the toilet to the sink, from the sink to the stove, from the stove to the table.

(5) Powdered eggs for breakfast. That was murder, too. But it was a fast, cheap meal, easy to prepare, and the ingredients didn't waste a lot of storage space. The only trouble was, he hated the way they tasted. Harry wished he had time to eat his breakfasts in a restaurant. He could afford the price, but he couldn't afford to wait in line more than a half-hour or so. His office schedule at the agency started promptly at ten-thirty. And he didn't get out until three-thirty; it was a long, hard five-hour day. Sometimes he wished he worked in the New Philly area, where a four-hour day was the rule. But he supposed that wouldn't mean any real saving in time, because he'd have to live further out. What was the population in New Philly now? Something like 63,000,000, wasn't it? Chicagee was much smaller — only 38,000,000, this year.

(6) *This* year. Harry shook his head and took a gulp of the Instantea. Yes, this year the population was 38,000,000, and the boundaries of the community extended north to what used to be the old Milwaukee and south past Gary. What would it be like *next* year, and the year following?

(7) Lately that question had begun to haunt Harry. He couldn't quite figure out why. After all, it was none of his business, really. He had a good job, security, a nice place just two hours from the Loop. He even drove his own car. What more could he ask?

9. This story is set sometime in the future. Which of the following clues confirms that this story is set in the future?

   (A) the number of rooms in his apartment
   (B) the population of Chicagee
   (C) the affordability of cars
   (D) the affordable price of a restaurant meal

10. This story was published in 1958. What image did Bloch have of the future?

(A) incredibly crowded

(B) suffering from food shortages

(C) well-organized commutes

(D) long working hours

11. Besides population numbers, how does the author build up the idea of a crowded world?

(A) descriptions of bad-tasting food

(B) communication using telescreens

(C) descriptions of enormous cities

(D) descriptions of long, hard workdays

12. Why does Harry sometimes wish he worked in the New Philly area?

(A) shorter commute times

(B) shorter working hours

(C) better pay

(D) better food

13. Why does Harry live in a one-room apartment when he could afford a two-room apartment?

(A) He likes the efficiency of the small space.

(B) His lady friends like the convenience of the apartment.

(C) He is not married.

(D) He can't afford a larger apartment.

14. What's the population Harry mentions for Chicagee?

(A) 38 million

(B) 63 million

(C) 38 billion

(D) 63 billion

15. Which of the following statements can be inferred about Harry from Paragraph 7?

(A) He feels more fortunate than others but still has vague worries.

(B) He doesn't like Chicagee and feels his life would be better in another city.

(C) He feels overwhelmed by life's challenges but still feels optimistic.

(D) He hates his life but feels that marriage will make his life better.

16. Which of the following details support the generalization that Harry believes that life is difficult and unsatisfying? Write the letters in the box. ☐

(A) travel on commutrains

(B) the flavor of his breakfast

(C) the price of meals in restaurants

(D) the taste of Instantea

Answers and explanations

1. **D. serious enough that it requires monitoring.** The text states that the comingling of the virus strains is serious enough to require monitoring. Now that a new area of possible comingling has been found, the text implies it, too, should be monitored. Choice (A) isn't supported by the text, and even though Choices (B) and (C) are possible, they're not as clear and important statements as Choice (D).

   TIP

   Your preparation for the science test can help you with RLA passages and questions like these, and vice versa. That gives you a leg up on both tests!

2. **D. North Pacific.** The text states that this finding shows the North Atlantic is as significant a melting pot for birds and avian flu as the North Pacific. Choice (B) isn't mentioned; and although *Eurasia* is mentioned, it isn't mentioned as a place where birds from Europe and North America mingle.

3. **C. It proved that avian flu viruses had mingled in Iceland.** According to the text, only this statement is true. The other statements are contradicted by information in the text.

4. **A. It can lead to a new, dangerous strain of avian flu.** The text states that the virus evolves readily and that the mingling of North American and Eurasian strains can lead to new varieties that are dangerous to humans. Cold viruses and flu viruses aren't the same, so Choice (B) has nothing to do with the topic of this text. Choices (C) and (D) are not supported by information in the passage.

5. **C. factual and straightforward.** The tone of the passage is very calm, very factual. It isn't *lighthearted*, *deeply concerned*, or *gloomy*.

6. **B. the H5N1 strain.** The text refers only to the H5N1 strain as a possible human flu. The term *bird flu* refers to the entire category of disease not just the version dangerous to humans. There's no mention in the text of an *H5 flu*, and *Eurasian avian flu* simply refers to one part of the world where many strains of avian flu originate.

7. **D. It shifts the focus from risk to humans to the need for continued monitoring.** Choice (D) is correct because the paragraph indicates that the situation currently doesn't pose a high risk to humans but should be further monitored. The other choices are not supported by information in the paragraph.

8. **Essential: B, C; Not Essential: A, D.** Choice (B) is one of the key findings of the study, and Choice (C) is relevant for public health around the world, so both statements are essential to the summary. The types of birds, the exact locations in Iceland, and the type of land where the birds gathered are less important, so (A) and (D) are not essential to the summary.

9. **B. the population of Chicagee.** The urban population listed is well beyond anything existing today. The other details are possible today and so do not indicate that the story is set in the future.

10. **A. incredibly crowded.** The overwhelming view that Bloch sees is a future of incredible overcrowding. There doesn't appear to be a food shortage based on the content of the story, so Choice (B) is wrong. Working hours appear to be shorter, so Choice (D) is also incorrect. And the passage indicates that the commutes are long and hard, so Choice (C) is incorrect.

11. **C. descriptions of enormous cities.** The author says that cities have expanded greatly from their original borders, which is an indication of massive population growth. The other details are mentioned in the passage but do not indicate that the population has grown so large.

12. **B. shorter working hours.** Harry states that he sometimes wishes he worked there because of the shorter working hours but doesn't say anything about better pay. The text also states that the commuting times would be longer there.

13. **C. He is not married.** The text mentions legal restrictions on accommodations. Harry would have to be married to be entitled to a two-room apartment. Harry states that he makes a good income, so money isn't an issue, which means that Choice (D) is incorrect. His lady friends claim to like the convenience, but Harry knows they're just being polite, which rules out Choice (B). He certainly doesn't like the small space, despite its efficiency, so Choice (A) is incorrect.

14. **A. 38 million.** The text states that the population is 38,000,000 people. The population of New Philly is 63,000,000, which makes Choice (B) incorrect. Choices (C) and (D) are too large.

15. **A. He feels more fortunate than others but still has vague worries.** The third and fourth sentences of the paragraph say that Harry feels fortunate for having a good job, security, and a nice home, yet he can't figure out what is haunting him about the future.

16. **A, B. travel on commutrains** and **the flavor of his breakfast.** The passage says that commutrains and powdered eggs are "murder," so Choices (A) and (B) support the generalization. Choice (C) is not possible because he can afford to eat in restaurants. The passage does not give information on the flavor of Instantea, so this choice does not support the generalization.

A Sample Extended Response Prompt

Your task: Analyze the arguments presented in the two passages. Then develop an argument in which you explain how one position is better supported than the other. In your response, include relevant and specific evidence from both passages to support your argument.

Remember, you don't have to agree with the position you consider the better-argued position.

You have 45 minutes to complete this task.

Passage One

In the Good Old SummerTime!

For most of us, setting our clocks forward one hour in March is a sure sign that spring is coming, followed by summer! After a long, hard winter, particularly in the cold northern states, summer is a welcome time. Kids are out of school, it may be time for a vacation, and we can barbecue, hike, and enjoy the great outdoors. It's time for patios, porches, parks, and backyards!

One of the big advantages of daylight savings time is that it gives us more time to enjoy the great outdoors in summer. Studies show that people are more active on summer evenings if they have an extra hour of daytime to enjoy. And because of the crisis of obesity in America, more exercise is better for everyone, and the country!

Daylight savings time has some other advantages, too. Traffic studies show that accidents go down during daylight savings time because of the longer daylight hours. And daylight savings time helps the economy, too, because longer hours of daylight in the afternoon encourage people to go out and spend. Malls, shopping centers, and downtowns are more likely to be filled when it's light outside.

So daylight savings time is really beneficial! We should definitely keep this longstanding practice so that everyone can reap the benefits.

Spring Forward, Fall Back — Far Back!

Daylight savings time is a relatively new idea that is now past its prime. Daylight savings time was started only during World War I. Its purpose was to reduce the consumption of important supplies, such as fuel and candles, by allowing for an extra hour of daylight each day. Later, it was reimposed to encourage shopping and outdoor activities in summer. However, this practice is now outmoded.

Studies show that the transition to daylight savings time costs our country billions as companies, computer systems, and schedules have to be adjusted twice a year on such a massive scale. Medical studies show that disrupted sleep patterns have all sorts of negative consequences. Heart attacks and strokes go up right after the switchover because of the related stress. And everyone's circadian rhythms are disrupted twice a year, which causes symptoms similar to jet lag. This also causes auto accidents to soar in the days after the transitions as groggy drivers get into needless traffic accidents. Workplace accidents increase, too, as sleep-deprived workers make careless mistakes. In addition, studies of workplaces show that productivity goes down in the days after the twice-annual changeovers. Orders are messed up, and work has to be redone as workers recover from disrupted rest patterns.

Daylight savings time has also lost the energy savings that once made it attractive. Because people nowadays run their air conditioners day and night, energy consumption will not be much affected.

Keeping daylight savings time is also bad for international business. Globally, fewer countries than ever before continue to observe daylight savings time. The European Union recently decided to do away with daylight savings time for just the reasons already mentioned. Each year, the U.S. airline industry loses an average of $150 million realigning schedules to those of countries that don't observe daylight savings time. All of the disruption puts the United States at a disadvantage with the rest of the world.

It's time for the United States to align with a growing number of countries around the world and abolish this annual folly. Families, health, and the economy will only benefit.

Sample response

Here's an example of a solid RLA Extended Response for the given prompt. Compare it to yours. Then review both against the following criteria that the GED Testing Service uses to evaluate your writing, as explained in Block 2.

Switching to and from daylight savings time each year has many pros and many cons. While some people may enjoy some benefits from the switchover, the argument that daylight savings time has outlived its usefulness makes the stronger case.

Changing to daylight savings time has a few advantages. People can get outdoors more, and the added daylight is nice for summer fun. But few people really take advantage of this extra time. Most of my friends go to indoor gyms all year, so the extra daylight doesn't make much difference. And to tell the truth, in the southern United States, where I live, it's too hot to exercise outside anymore, as summer temperatures have increased due to global warming. As the article states, people just stay inside in cool, air-conditioned comfort.

There are many more negatives to daylight savings time. The changeover has all kinds of costs. It has very bad effects on our health, including a big increase in heart attacks, as reported in some medical studies. Other medical studies show that people get into more car accidents. Accidents and errors go up at work, too, which is costly. Daylight savings time also puts us out of kilter with the rest of the world. Fewer countries observe it now than before, so American businesses have to make a lot of effort to stay in sync. My company buys parts from other countries. Each year, we have trouble ordering parts around daylight savings time because we are on different schedules. Daylight savings time gets airline schedules out of whack, too, which costs those companies billions of dollars.

As you can see, although daylight savings time was helpful in a bygone day, the changeover twice a year costs Americans billions of dollars in needless expense, lost wages, poor health, and inconvenience, with few clear benefits to people's lives.

RLA Grammar and Language

The questions in the Grammar and Language component of the RLA test are doubly important because understanding and using correct grammar adds to your overall score on the RLA test and also counts toward your score on the Extended Response item. One of the important things about proper grammar is that it sounds and reads well. These questions give you an opportunity to develop your ear and eye for proper sentences.

For the questions in this section, pay special attention to the mechanics of writing, spelling, and grammar. Work carefully, but don't spend too much time on any one question. Be sure to answer every question. You can find complete answers and explanations for these items later in this section.

Questions

Questions 1–10 refer to the following executive summary.

Dry-Cleaning and Laundering Industry Adjustment Committee Report on the Local Labor Market Partnership Project

Executive Summary

Over the past two years, the Dry-Cleaning and Laundering Industry Adjustment Committee has worked hard to become a cohesive [Select... ▼] on assessing and addressing the human resource implications associated with changes in the fabricare industry. As of August, the Committee has an active membership of [Select... ▼] 15 individuals involved in all aspects of the project. The Committee has taken responsibility for undertaking actions that will benefit this large, highly fragmented [Select... ▼] great difficulty speaking with one voice.

During the initial period that the Committee was in [Select... ▼] work focused on reaching out to and building a relationship with key individuals within the industry. One of its first steps [Select... ▼] was to undertake a Needs Assessment Survey within the industry.

During the first year, the Committee explored ways of meeting the needs identified in the Needs Assessment [Select... ▼] raising the profile of the industry and offering on-site training programs, particularly in the areas of spotting and pressing. A great deal of feasibility work [Select... ▼] yet each possible training solution proved to be extremely difficult and costly to implement.

As the Committee moved into its second [Select... ▼] officially established a joint project with the National Fabricare Association to achieve goals in three priority areas: mentorship, training, and profile building.

During this [Select... ▼] effort and vision has gone into achieving the goals established by the Industry Adjustment Committee and the Association. The new priority areas have provided an opportunity for the industry to take these [Select... ▼]

- Introduce technology
- Build capacity and knowledge
- Enhance skills
- Build partnerships and networks

1. Over the past two years, the Dry-Cleaning and Laundering Industry Adjustment Committee has worked hard to become a cohesive [Select... ▼] on assessing and addressing the human resource implications associated with changes in the fabricare industry.

   (A) group and one which has focused

   (B) group. One which has focused

   (C) group, and one which has focused

   (D) group focused

2. As of August, the Committee has an active membership of [Select... ▼] 15 individuals involved in all aspects of the project.

   (A) most over

   (B) moreover

   (C) over than

   (D) more than

3. The Committee has taken responsibility for undertaking actions that will benefit this large, highly fragmented [Select... ▼] great difficulty speaking with one voice.

   (A) industry which has

   (B) industry, which have

   (C) industry, who has

   (D) industry, which has

4. During the initial period that the Committee was in [Select... ▼] work focused on reaching out to and building a relationship with key individuals within the industry.

   (A) existence, it's

   (B) existence, its

   (C) existence its

   (D) existence; its

5. One of its first steps [Select... ▼] to undertake a Needs Assessment Survey within the industry.

   (A) was

   (B) had been

   (C) were

   (D) would have been

6. During the first year, the Committee explored ways of meeting the needs identified in the Needs Assessment [Select... ▼] raising the profile of the industry and offering on-site training programs, particularly in the areas of spotting and pressing.

   (A) Survey and they included,

   (B) Survey. These needs included

   (C) Survey, and they included

   (D) Survey they included

7. A great deal of feasibility work [Select... ▼] yet each possible training solution proved to be extremely difficult and costly to implement.

(A) were undertaken during this phase

(B) was undertook during this phase

(C) was undertaken, during this phase

(D) was undertaken during this phase,

8. As the Committee moved into its second [Select... ▼] officially established a joint project with the National Fabricare Association to achieve goals in three priority areas: mentorship, training, and profile building.

(A) year: it

(B) year it

(C) year; it

(D) year, it

9. During this [Select... ▼] effort and vision has gone into achieving the goals established by the Industry Adjustment Committee and the Association.

(A) passed year, many

(B) past year, much

(C) past year much

(D) passed year, much

10. The new priority areas have provided an opportunity for the industry to take these [Select... ▼]

- Introduce technology

- Build capacity and knowledge

- Enhance skills

- Build partnerships and networks

(A) actions

(B) actions;

(C) actions,

(D) actions:

Questions 11–20 refer to the following description of an adult education class at a local community college.

Adult Learning 265: Prior Learning Assessment and Recognition

This course is based on a Prior Learning Assessment and Recognition (PLAR) [Select... ▼] on successful completion of the GED test. [Select... ▼] candidates are guided through the creation of a portfolio, which can be evaluated by a college for admission or advanced standing. This is an opportunity for adults, who have learned in non-formal as well as formal venues, to document and assess [Select... ▼] prior learning. The course is [Select... ▼]. It is not meant for every applicant.

[Select... ▼] should be directed to remedial programs before beginning such a rigorous course. [Select... ▼] in a pre-test may be advised to arrange immediately to take one or more of the GED tests. This course is meant for candidates who will gain from [Select... ▼] do not require extensive teaching.

This course is designed to help adult learners gain credit for [Select... ▼] prior learning in preparation for post-secondary study. Students will learn methods for documenting prior knowledge, [Select... ▼] reacquainted with educational environments. Through the use of assessment tools and [Select... ▼] will gain a realistic understanding of their levels of competence, personal strengths, weaknesses, and learning styles.

11. This course is based on a Prior Learning Assessment and Recognition (PLAR) [Select... ▼] on successful completion of the GED test.

   (A) model, and focuses

   (B) model and focuses

   (C) model it focuses

   (D) model, it focuses

12. [Select... ▼] candidates are guided through the creation of a portfolio, which can be evaluated by a college for admission or advanced standing.

   (A) In addition,

   (B) However,

   (C) Nevertheless,

   (D) In contrast,

13. This is an opportunity for adults, who have learned in non-formal as well as formal venues, to document and assess [Select... ▼] prior learning.

   (A) their

   (B) there

   (C) they're

   (D) themselves

14. The course is [Select... ▼].

   (A) intents and concentrated

   (B) intents and concentrate

   (C) intense and concentrate

   (D) intense and concentrated

15. [Select... ▼] should be directed to remedial programs before beginning such a rigorous course.

   (A) Candidates who score low in the pre-test,

   (B) Candidates, who score low in the pre-test

   (C) Candidates who score low in the pre-test

   (D) Candidates, who score low in the pre-test;

16. [Select... ▼] in a pre-test may be advised to arrange immediately to take one or more of the GED tests.

   (A) Extremely those who score well

   (B) Those who score well extremely

   (C) Those who score extremely well

   (D) Those extremely who score well

17. This course is meant for candidates who will gain from [Select... ▾] do not require extensive teaching.

   (A) review and remediation. But

   (B) review, and remediation but

   (C) review, and remediation but,

   (D) review and remediation but

18. This course is designed to help adult learners gain credit for [Select... ▾] prior learning in preparation for post-secondary study.

   (A) their

   (B) his or her

   (C) our

   (D) my

19. Students will learn methods for documenting prior knowledge, [Select... ▾] reacquainted with educational environments.

   (A) will develop academic skills while becoming

   (B) will develop academic skills, and becoming

   (C) will develop academic skills, and will become

   (D) develop academic skills, and will become

20. Through the use of assessment tools and [Select... ▾] will gain a realistic understanding of their levels of competence, personal strengths, weaknesses, and learning styles.

   (A) counseling; students

   (B) counseling. Students

   (C) counseling students

   (D) counseling, students

Answers and explanations

1. **D. group focused.** With this choice, you create a concise sentence and avoid the overly wordy and awkward sentence in Choice (A). Options (B) and (C) introduce new errors.

2. **D. more than.** Choice (D) uses *more than* correctly to refer to quantities. The other choices introduce additional errors.

3. **D. industry, which has.** Choice (D) is correct because a comma is needed to indicate that this relative clause contains non-essential information. Therefore, Choice (A) is incorrect. Choice (B) introduces a subject-verb agreement error. *Industry* is the word that *which* refers to, so a singular verb is required. Choice (C) uses an incorrect pronoun; *which* is required because it refers to a thing, *industry*, not a person.

4. **B. existence, its.** Choice (B) is correct because the possessive form of *it, its,* is needed here, not the contraction for *it is: it's* (Choice A). There is no reason to remove the comma (Choice C) or replace it with a semicolon (Choice D).

5. **A. was.** In this sentence, the subject of the verb is the singular subject *One*, so the singular form of the verb, *was*, is needed.

TIP

Are you thinking that I made a mistake in the preceding sentence? Well, I didn't. The noun that is closest to the verb is not always the subject. The prepositional phrase *of its first steps* doesn't determine how the noun and verb agree. *One*, a singular noun, is subject of the sentence and, therefore, needs *was*, not *were*.

6. **B. Survey. These needs included.** This option creates two concise sentences instead of one long, rambling one, as in the other options.

TIP

When answering Grammar and Language questions or writing your essay, keep in mind that sentences shouldn't be so long that you have to take multiple breaths just to read them aloud. Short sentences are easier to read and understand and are less likely to need all sorts of pesky punctuation.

7. **D. was undertaken during this phase,** A comma after *phase* is required because this a compound sentence joined by the conjunction *yet*. A compound sentence needs a comma before the conjunction. Therefore, the remaining options, which omit this punctuation, are incorrect. In addition, there is no reason to use *were* instead of *was* (Choice A) or to change *undertaken* to *undertook* (Choice B). Choice (C) adds an extra comma that is not needed.

A *compound sentence* contains two independent clauses or thoughts. The clauses are joined by a comma and a conjunction such as *and, but,* or *yet*.

8. **D. year, it.** This choice is correct because a comma is needed to separate the introductory clause starting with *As* from the rest of the sentence. Replacing the comma with another punctuation mark (Choices A and C) or removing it (Choice B) are both incorrect.

9. **B. past year, much.** Choice (B) is correct because it avoids the homonym spelling error (*passed/past*) in Choices (A) and (D). There is no reason to use *many* instead of *much*, which is another reason Choice (A) is incorrect. A comma is needed after *year*, so Choice (C) is incorrect.

WARNING

Homonyms are two or more words that sound alike or are spelled alike but have different meanings. The word *passed* is a verb and means "went by," as in "she passed the other car," or "completed a test successfully," as in "he passed the GED." The word *past* is a noun and means "in times gone by, in a prior time," as in, "In the past, there were no computers." The GED Grammar and Language component frequently tests your ability to use the correct homonym, so keep an eye out for them. Writing the wrong homonym in your essay can also contribute to a lower score.

10. **D. actions:** The clause needs a colon at the end to introduce the list that follows (Choice D). Therefore, the other choices are incorrect.

11. **B. model and focuses.** Option (B) is correct because *and* joins two verbs (*is based* and *focuses*), not two clauses, and so does not need a comma. Therefore, Option (A) is incorrect. Option (C) creates a run-on sentence. Option (D) creates a comma splice.

Two independent clauses should be joined by a comma and a conjunction, such as *and* or *but*. When you join two clauses with just a comma, it's called a *comma splice*. When you join them without a conjunction and a comma, it's called a *run-on sentence*. Look at these examples.

Correct: This course is based on a Prior Learning Assessment and Recognition (PLAR) model, **and** it focuses on successful completion of the GED test.

Run-On: This course is based on a Prior Learning Assessment and Recognition (PLAR) model it focuses on successful completion of the GED test.

Comma Splice: This course is based on a Prior Learning Assessment and Recognition (PLAR) model, it focuses on successful completion of the GED test.

12. A. In addition, This sentence adds an idea to the previous one, so the best transitional phrase is in Choice (A). When one of these phrases is at the beginning of a sentence, it's followed by a comma.

Not sure about commas? Check out *English Grammar For Dummies,* 2nd Edition, by Geraldine Woods (Wiley) for the lowdown on this tricky punctuation mark.

13. A. their. *Their* is possessive (showing belonging) and is the correct choice in this sentence.

The homonyms *there, their,* and *they're* probably trip up more people than any other homonyms, and these tricky words are frequently tested on the GED RLA test. Before test day, be sure you know the difference!

14. D. intense and concentrated. *Intense* and *concentrated* are synonyms used in this sentence for emphasis, but in Choices (A) and (B), *intense* is replaced with a close homonym, *intents*. *Intents* means, "plans or purposes." *Concentrated* is an adjective, so it is used correctly in Choices (A) and (D). There is no reason to use *concentrate*, as in Choices (B) and (C), which is a verb (*to concentrate*) or a noun (as in *orange juice concentrate*). Only Choice (D) uses both correct words.

15. C. Candidates who score low in the pre-test. The clause *who score low in the pre-test* is an *essential relative clause*, which means it refers to a specific noun — *candidates*, in this case — and specifies something about the noun that the sentence needs in order to make sense to readers. Essential relative clauses aren't separated by commas because they're an integral part of the sentence.

Contrast the *essential* relative clause with the *non-essential* relative clause, which adds information about the noun that isn't essential to the meaning of the sentence. If you remove a non-essential clause from the sentence, you can still fully understand the meaning of the sentence. Non-essential relative clauses require commas to separate them from the sentence. For example, consider the following sentence: "The teacher, who had bright red hair, reviewed the grammar rule with the class." The information between the commas (who had bright red hair) isn't essential to the meaning of the sentence.

16. C. Those who score extremely well. *Those who score extremely well* is the best order of the words. *Extremely*, an adverb, is best placed before the word it modifies, which is *well*.

17. D. review and remediation but. Commas are not needed in this series of nouns joined by *and* and *but*. Therefore, Options (B) and (C) are incorrect. Option (A) creates a sentence fragment.

A *sentence fragment* is a group of words with an initial capital letter and a final period but that is not a complete sentence. A fragment lacks a subject or a verb. You can avoid a fragment by giving it a complete subject or a complete verb or by joining it to another sentence using correct conjunction (such as *and* or *but),* punctuation, and capitalization.

18. A. their. This item assesses your ability to choose pronouns that agree with their antecedent — the noun they refer to. In this case, the antecedent is *adult learners,* so *their,* Choice (A), is correct.

19. C. will develop academic skills, and will become. Choice (C) puts the three things students will do (learn methods, develop skills, and become reacquainted) in the same grammatical form, verb phrases. This is called *parallel structure*.

Parallel structure makes writing clear and easy to follow because similar ideas are expressed in the same grammatical form. Parallel structure is frequently tested on the GED. Here are some examples of different kinds of parallel structure:

The GED has tests on math, language arts, social studies, and science. (nouns)

They studied academic content, reviewed test-taking skills, and learned computer skills. (verb phrases)

The students studied in the library, the teachers worked in their classrooms, and the administrators sat in their offices. (clauses)

20. **D. counseling, students.** A comma is needed to set off this phrase from the rest of the sentence. Therefore, Choices (A) and (C) are incorrect. Choice (B) creates a sentence fragment.

Social Studies Sample Questions

The official Social Studies test consists mainly of multiple-choice items but also has other question types explained in Block 1. *Remember:* On the real test, you can use the on-screen calculator (or your own calculator if you take the test at a testing center).

Questions

Questions 1 and 2 refer to the following excerpt from a U.S. government publication.

Democracies fall into two basic categories, direct and representative. In a direct democracy, citizens, without the intermediary of elected or appointed officials, can participate in making public decisions. Such a system is clearly most practical with relatively small numbers of people — in a community organization, tribal council, or the local unit of a labor union, for example — where members can meet in a single room to discuss issues and arrive at decisions by consensus or majority vote.

Some U.S. states, in addition, place "propositions" and "referendums" — mandated changes of law — or possible recall of elected officials on ballots during state elections. These practices are forms of direct democracy, expressing the will of a large population. Many practices may have elements of direct democracy. In Switzerland, many important political decisions on issues, including public health, energy, and employment, are subject to a vote by the country's citizens. And some might argue that the Internet is creating new forms of direct democracy, as it empowers political groups to raise money for their causes by appealing directly to like-minded citizens.

However, today, as in the past, the most common form of democracy, whether for a town of 50,000 or a nation of 50 million, is representative democracy, in which citizens elect officials to make political decisions, formulate laws, and administer programs for the public good.

1. The federal government of the United States is an example of a ⬚⬚⬚⬚⬚ (direct or representative) democracy.

2. Which of the following is an example of allowing the population as a whole to vote on an issue?
   (A) a vote on issuing library bonds
   (B) the election of a local mayor
   (C) the election of the president
   (D) a school board election

Questions 3 and 4 refer to the following excerpt from a U.S. government publication.

In a democracy, government is only one thread in the social fabric of many and varied public and private institutions, legal forums, political parties, organizations, and associations. This diversity is called pluralism, and it assumes that the many organized groups and institutions in a democratic society do not depend upon government for their existence, legitimacy, or authority. Most democratic societies have thousands of private organizations, some local, some national. Many of them serve a mediating role between individuals and society's complex social and governmental institutions, filling roles not given to the government and offering individuals opportunities to become part of their society without being in government.

In an authoritarian society, virtually all such organizations would be controlled, licensed, watched, or otherwise accountable to the government. In a democracy, the powers of the government are, by law, clearly defined and sharply limited. As a result, private organizations are largely free of government control. In this busy private realm of democratic society, citizens can explore the possibilities of peaceful self-fulfillment and the responsibilities of belonging to a community — free of the potentially heavy hand of the state or the demand that they adhere to views held by those with influence or power, or by the majority.

3. Which of the following is an example of an authoritarian society?

   (A) Canada

   (B) Kingdom of Sweden

   (C) the former USSR

   (D) the Republic of Korea (South Korea)

4. All United States citizens have the right to elect

   (A) their senator.

   (B) Supreme Court justices.

   (C) cabinet secretaries.

   (D) army generals.

Questions 5–9 refer to the following excerpt from U.S. History For Dummies, *by Steve Wiegand (Wiley).*

Partly because of error and partly because of wishful thinking, Columbus estimated the distance to the Indies at approximately 2,500 miles, which was about 7,500 miles short. But after a voyage of about five weeks, he and his crew, totaling 90 men, did find land at around 2:00 a.m. on October 12, 1492. It was an island in the Bahamas, which he called San Salvador. The timing of the discovery was good; it came even as the crews of the *Nina, Pinta,* and *Santa Maria* were muttering about a mutiny.

Columbus next sailed to Cuba, where he found a few spices and little gold. Sailing on to an island he called Hispaniola (today's Dominican Republic and Haiti), the *Santa Maria* hit a reef on Christmas Eve, 1492. Columbus abandoned the ship, set up a trading outpost he called Navidad, left some men to operate it, and sailed back to Spain in his other two ships.

So enthusiastically did people greet the news of his return that on his second voyage to Hispaniola, Columbus had 17 ships and more than 1,200 men. But this time he ran into more than a little disappointment. Natives had wiped out his trading post after his men became too grabby with the local gold and the local women. Worse, most of the men he brought with him had come only for gold and other riches, and they didn't care about setting up a permanent colony. Because of the lack of treasures, they soon wanted to go home. And the natives lost interest in the newcomers after the novelty of the Spanish trinkets wore off.

5. By how much was Columbus in error in guessing the distance to the Indies? Write the answer in the box. ☐

6. On what date did Columbus arrive in the Bahamas?

    (A) October 2, 1492

    (B) October 12, 1492

    (C) December 12, 1493

    (D) Christmas Eve, 1492

7. Why did so many people want to sail with Columbus on his second trip?

    (A) They were eager to settle new lands.

    (B) They wanted adventure.

    (C) They had heard stories about amazing cities.

    (D) They had heard stories of the gold Columbus had found.

8. Why did Columbus cut his first voyage short?

    (A) The *Santa Maria* had hit a reef and sank.

    (B) His men were ready to mutiny.

    (C) He had completed his task by setting up a small colony.

    (D) Disease decimated his crew.

9. Columbus's goal was to sail to the continent of ☐.

Questions 10 and 11 refer to the following excerpt from U.S. History For Dummies, *by Steve Wiegand (Wiley).*

On his second trip to the Americas in 1493, Columbus stopped by the Canary Islands and picked up some sugar cane cuttings. He planted them on Hispaniola, and they thrived. In 1516, the first sugar grown in the New World was presented to King Carlos I of Spain. By 1531, it was as commercially important to the Spanish colonial economy as gold.

Planters soon discovered a by-product as well. The juice left over after the sugar was pressed out of the cane and crystallized was called *melasas* by the Spanish (and *molasses* by the English). Mixing this juice with water and leaving it out in the sun created a potent and tasty fermented drink. They called it *rum* — perhaps after the word for sugar cane, *Saccharum officinarum*. The stuff was great for long sea voyages because it didn't go bad.

Sugar and rum became so popular that sugar plantations mushroomed all over the Caribbean.

10. What is molasses?

    (A) juice pressed out of sugar cane

    (B) leftover juice after sugar was pressed out of the cane

    (C) sugar cane mixed with water

    (D) *Saccharum officinarum*

11. How many years did it take before the first sugar cane grown in the New World was presented to the king of Spain?

    (A) 33 years

    (B) 23 years

    (C) 13 years

    (D) 1 year

Educational Attainment of the Population 25 Years and Over, by Selected Characteristics: 2019
(Numbers in thousands. Civilian noninstitutionalized population.[1])

Both sexes	Total	None - 8th grade	9th - 11th grade	High school graduate	Some college, no degree	Associate's degree	Bachelor's degree	Master's degree	Professional degree	Doctoral degree
Total	2,21,478	8,603	13,372	62,259	34,690	22,738	49,937	22,214	3,136	4,529
Marital Status										
Married, spouse present	1,26,768	4,476	6,069	32,493	18,378	13,410	31,280	15,096	2,240	3,327
Married, spouse absent, not separated	3,633	294	339	1,063	468	293	692	355	39	89
Separated	4,643	342	585	1,618	759	454	617	206	34	28
Widowed	14,852	1,218	1,414	5,459	2,411	1,284	1,960	872	100	134
Divorced	25,235	697	1,645	7,790	4,815	3,038	4,707	1,983	235	327
Never married	46,348	1,576	3,320	13,836	7,858	4,259	10,681	3,704	488	625
Household Relationship										
Family householder	80,502	2,608	4,497	20,288	13,436	8,923	18,642	9,004	1,232	1,872
Married, spouse present	61,073	1,865	2,683	14,226	9,613	6,630	15,539	7,705	1,097	1,714
Other family householder	19,429	742	1,814	6,062	3,823	2,293	3,103	1,299	136	157
Nonfamily householder	41,973	1,494	2,646	11,553	7,323	4,281	9,321	4,045	513	795
Living alone	34,952	1,333	2,284	9,880	6,149	3,552	7,347	3,306	432	668
Living with nonrelatives	7,020	161	362	1,673	1,174	729	1,974	739	82	127
Relative of householder	86,578	3,972	5,399	26,395	12,019	8,459	19,187	8,181	1,266	1,699
Spouse	61,000	2,029	2,897	16,692	8,220	6,379	14,984	7,117	1,102	1,579
Other	25,577	1,943	2,501	9,703	3,799	2,081	4,203	1,064	163	121
Nonrelative	12,426	529	830	4,022	1,912	1,074	2,786	985	125	162
Citizenship, Nativity, and Year of Entry										
Native born	1,81,283	2,767	9,420	52,024	31,198	19,984	41,686	18,120	2,568	3,515
Native parentage[2]	1,63,644	2,382	8,627	47,620	28,126	18,083	37,290	16,212	2,208	3,096
Foreign or mixed parentage[3]	17,639	385	793	4,404	3,072	1,901	4,396	1,907	361	419
Foreign born	40,195	5,836	3,952	10,235	3,492	2,754	8,250	4,095	568	1,014
Naturalized citizen	20,751	1,856	1,427	5,263	2,246	1,794	5,036	2,102	394	634
Not a citizen	19,444	3,980	2,525	4,972	1,245	960	3,214	1,993	174	380
Year of entry										
2010 or later	7,963	766	560	1,845	568	446	2,145	1,329	96	207
2000-2009	10,252	1,636	1,224	2,732	747	620	1,943	929	162	259
1990-1999	9,796	1,413	1,086	2,578	822	771	1,870	876	138	242
1980-1989	6,414	1,064	692	1,597	684	464	1,208	480	82	142
1970-1979	3,446	653	245	807	356	238	672	311	51	112
Before 1970	2,324	303	146	676	314	216	412	168	38	52
Labor Force Status										
Employed	1,37,478	3,597	5,726	34,453	20,731	15,235	35,820	16,050	2,425	3,440
Unemployed	4,531	169	464	1,403	860	450	809	293	45	37
Not in civilian labor force	79,470	4,837	7,182	26,403	13,099	7,053	13,307	5,871	666	1,052
Occupation (Employed Civilians Only)	1,37,478	3,597	5,726	34,453	20,731	15,235	35,820	16,050	2,425	3,440
Management, business, and financial occupations	25,465	170	329	3,412	3,315	2,342	10,185	4,848	323	540
Professional and related occupations	34,622	37	117	2,204	2,575	3,677	12,658	8,720	1,914	2,721
Service occupations	20,981	1,191	1,816	7,926	3,913	2,557	2,940	525	61	52
Sales and related occupations	12,598	148	447	3,450	2,388	1,390	3,908	787	36	44
Office and administrative occupations	15,040	95	331	4,586	3,672	2,122	3,385	768	30	51
Farming, forestry, and fishing occupations	929	256	140	314	88	54	62	15	-	-
Construction and extraction occupations	7,283	741	864	3,238	1,016	691	641	69	18	5
Installation, maintenance, and repair occupations	4,132	119	250	1,751	816	783	370	36	6	2
Production occupations	7,705	490	621	3,496	1,422	850	699	105	13	8
Transportation and material moving occupations	8,723	349	811	4,078	1,526	769	972	178	23	17
Industry (Employed Civilians Only)	1,37,478	3,597	5,726	34,453	20,731	15,235	35,820	16,050	2,425	3,440
Agricultural, forestry, fishing, and hunting	2,017	297	194	657	254	193	317	80	6	18
Mining	704	14	33	263	115	60	142	65	-	11
Construction	9,849	775	982	3,948	1,458	956	1,384	289	39	17
Manufacturing	14,450	517	746	4,663	2,203	1,608	3,280	1,212	49	172
Wholesale and retail trade	15,893	307	798	5,240	3,155	1,794	3,601	771	81	146
Transportation and utilities	8,009	175	403	2,972	1,676	959	1,447	327	27	25
Information	2,455	11	31	391	385	218	985	390	12	31
Financial activities	9,847	43	120	1,621	1,495	979	4,036	1,312	120	122
Professional and business services	17,821	448	520	3,009	2,183	1,549	6,119	2,689	724	579
Educational and health services	33,060	222	670	5,019	3,756	4,281	9,078	6,895	1,102	2,037
Leisure and hospitality	9,980	503	755	3,299	1,801	928	2,143	500	34	17
Other services	6,590	255	400	2,223	1,018	862	1,171	515	57	90
Public administration	6,802	29	73	1,147	1,232	847	2,117	1,005	176	175

Source: Adapted from U.S. Census Bureau

12. How many foreign-born individuals who entered the United States after 2010 were high school graduates? [   ] Write your answer in thousands.

13. Comparing educational attainment of employed and unemployed individuals, the data shows a [   ] (high *or* low) correlation between education and employment.

Question 14 refers to the following graph.

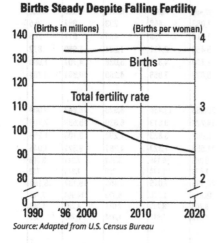

Births Steady Despite Falling Fertility

Source: Adapted from U.S. Census Bureau

14. The graph shows the total number of births around the entire world in one year as compared to the total fertility rate (TFR). The graph shows a steady decline in the TFR — that is, the number of children born to the average woman — yet the total number of births in the world remains the same. Why is that?

(A) Birth rates have fallen in Europe, the United States, and Japan.

(B) The TFR counts only live births.

(C) The growing world population means that each woman having fewer children is offset by the fact that there are more women to have children.

(D) In China, families are again allowed to have more than one child.

Questions 15–17 refer to the following excerpt from The Declaration of Independence, 1776.

After a long list of grievances, the Declaration of Independence concludes with these words.

In every stage of these Oppressions We have Petitioned for Redress in the most humble terms: Our repeated Petitions have been answered only by repeated injury. A Prince whose character is thus marked by every act which may define a Tyrant, is unfit to be the ruler of a free people.

Nor have We been wanting in attentions to our British brethren. We have warned them from time to time of attempts by their legislature to extend an unwarrantable jurisdiction over us. We have reminded them of the circumstances of our emigration and settlement here. We have appealed to their native justice and magnanimity, and we have conjured them by the ties of our common kindred to disavow these usurpations, which would inevitably interrupt our connections and correspondence. They too have been deaf to the voice of justice and of consanguinity. We must, therefore, acquiesce in the necessity, which denounces our Separation, and hold them, as we hold the rest of mankind, Enemies in War, in Peace Friends.

We, therefore, the Representatives of the united States of America, in General Congress, Assembled, appealing to the Supreme Judge of the world for the rectitude of our intentions, do, in the Name, and by Authority of the good People of these Colonies, solemnly publish and declare, That these United Colonies are, and of Right ought to be Free and Independent States; that they are Absolved from all Allegiance to the British Crown, and that all political connection between them and the State of Great Britain, is and ought to be totally dissolved; and that as Free and Independent States, they have full Power to levy War, conclude Peace, contract Alliances, establish Commerce, and to do all other Acts and Things which Independent States may of right do. And for the support of this Declaration, with a firm reliance on the protection of divine Providence, we mutually pledge to each other our Lives, our Fortunes and our sacred Honor.

15. Why did the authors of the Declaration of Independence believe the king was a tyrant?

    (A) The king's only answer to their complaints was more repression.

    (B) Appeals to British parliament failed.

    (C) The king had taxed them without representation.

    (D) They rejected the king's authority.

16. How did the authors feel about British parliament making laws for the colonies?

    (A) The laws were usurpations.

    (B) The laws were magnanimous.

    (C) The laws are examples of justice and consanguinity.

    (D) The parliament heeded the authors' concerns.

17. Why is the word *united* in "united States of America" not also capitalized?

    (A) The states viewed themselves as independent entities.

    (B) The representatives saw themselves as belonging to one country.

    (C) This Congress was a meeting of independent states united for action.

    (D) The authors of the Declaration were following old-fashioned rules for writing.

Questions 18 and 19 refer to the following passage from U.S. History For Dummies, *by Steve Wiegand (Wiley).*

By 1787, it was apparent to many leaders that the Articles of Confederation needed an overhaul, or the union of states would eventually fall apart. So Congress agreed to call a convention of delegates from each state to try to fix things. The first of the delegates (selected by state legislatures) to arrive in Philadelphia in May 1787 was James Madison, a 36-year-old scholar and politician from Virginia who was so frail, he couldn't serve in the army during the Revolution. Madison had so many ideas on how to fix things, he couldn't wait to get started.

Not everyone else was in such a hurry. Although the convention was supposed to begin May 15, it wasn't until May 25 that enough of the delegates chosen by the state legislatures showed up to have a quorum. Rhode Island never did send anyone.

Eventually, 55 delegates took part. Notable by their absence were some of the leading figures of the recent rebellion against England: Thomas Jefferson was in France, Thomas Paine was in England, Sam Adams and John Hancock weren't selected to go, and Patrick Henry refused.

18. What was the name of the original constitution of the United States?

   (A) the Articles of Confederation
   (B) the Constitution of the Confederation
   (C) the Declaration of Independence
   (D) the Declaration of the Rights of Man

19. Why was James Madison especially important to this convention?

   (A) He was eager to get started.
   (B) He represented one of the southern states, which made him very important.
   (C) He had never served in the military.
   (D) He had many ideas on how to fix things.

Questions 20–22 are based on this excerpt from a speech by James Madison on the ratification of the new Constitution of the United States.

What has brought on other nations those immense debts, under the pressure of which many of them labor? Not the expenses of their governments, but war. . . . How is it possible a war could be supported without money or credit? And would it be possible for government to have credit, without having the power of raising money? No, it would be impossible for any government, in such a case, to defend itself. Then, I say, sir, that it is necessary to establish funds for extraordinary exigencies, and give this power to the general government; for the utter inutility of previous requisitions on the States is too well known. Would it be possible for those countries, whose finances and revenues are carried to the highest perfection, to carry on the operations of government on great emergencies, such as the maintenance of a war, without an uncontrolled power of raising money? Has it not been necessary for Great Britain, notwithstanding the facility of the collection of her taxes, to have recourse very often to this and other extraordinary methods of procuring money? Would not her public credit have been ruined, if it was known that her power to raise money was limited?. . . [N]o government can exist unless its powers extend to make provisions for every contingency.

If we were actually attacked by a powerful nation, and our general government had not the power of raising money, but depended solely on requisitions, our condition would be truly deplorable: if the revenues of this commonwealth were to depend on twenty distinct authorities, it would be impossible for it to carry on its operations.

20. According to Madison, what was the major reason for allowing the government to raise revenue?

   (A) to provide a single economic market
   (B) to have the ability to fund extraordinary exigencies
   (C) to limit the power of the states
   (D) to limit the power of the national government

21. What was Madison referring to by "the utter inutility of previous requisitions on the States is too well known"?

   (A) Under the Articles of Confederation, it was easy to convince all the states to contribute money.
   (B) Under the Articles of Confederation, the government had very unlimited powers to tax.
   (C) Under the Articles of Confederation, the states controlled the government.
   (D) Under the Articles of Confederation, the government had only very limited powers to tax.

22. How many states were part of the original Confederation? [   ]

Questions 23–25 refer to the following passage, excerpted from "A Look Back . . . The Black Dispatches: Intelligence During the Civil War," a CIA Feature Story (www.cia.gov).

William A. Jackson

African-Americans who could serve as agents-in-place were a great asset to the Union. They could provide information about the enemy's plans instead of reporting how the plans were carried out. William A. Jackson was one such agent-in-place who provided valuable intelligence straight from Confederate President Jefferson Davis.

Jackson served as a coachman to Davis. As a servant in Davis' home, Jackson overheard discussions the president had with his military leadership. His first report of Confederate plans and intentions was in May 1862 when he crossed into Union lines. While there are no records of the specific intelligence Jackson reported, it is known that it was important enough to be sent straight to the War Department in Washington.

Harriet Tubman

When it comes to the Civil War and the fight to end slavery, Harriet Tubman is an icon. She was not only a conductor of the Underground Railroad, but also a spy for the Union.

In 1860, she took her last trip on the Underground Railroad, bringing friends and family to freedom safely. After the trip, Tubman decided to contribute to the war effort by caring for and feeding the many slaves who had fled the Union-controlled areas.

A year later, the Union Army asked Tubman to gather a network of spies among the black men in the area. Tubman also was tasked with leading expeditions to gather intelligence. She reported her information to a Union officer commanding the Second South Carolina Volunteers, a black unit involved in guerrilla warfare activities.

After learning of Tubman's capability as a spy, Gen. David Hunter, commander of all Union forces in the area, requested that Tubman personally guide a raiding party up the Combahee River in South Carolina. Tubman was well prepared for the raid because she had key information about Confederate positions along the shore and had discovered where they placed torpedoes (barrels filled with gunpowder) in the water. On the morning of June 1, 1863, Tubman led Col. James Montgomery and his men in the attack. The expedition hit hard. They set fires and destroyed buildings so they couldn't be used by the Confederate forces. The raiders freed 750 slaves.

The raid along the Combahee River, In addition to her activities with the Underground Railroad, made a significant contribution to the Union cause. When Tubman died in 1913, she was honored with a full military funeral in recognition for work during the war.

23. What made William Jackson an excellent intelligence source?

(A) He was an African-American.

(B) He had military experience.

(C) He worked in the home of Jefferson Davis.

(D) He was in direct contact with Washington, D.C.

24. What is Harriet Tubman best known for?

    (A) the Underground Railroad

    (B) the drinking gourd song

    (C) being a guerilla leader

    (D) spying on the president of the Confederacy

25. Harriet Tubman led a raid on ⬚ in South Carolina.

    (A) the Combahee River

    (B) Montgomery

    (C) Union-controlled areas

    (D) Atlanta

Questions 26 and 27 refer to the following excerpt from U.S. History For Dummies, *by Steve Wiegand (Wiley).*

Despite conflict in war, civilians and soldiers around the world had at least one thing in common in 1918 — a killer flu. Erroneously dubbed "Spanish Influenza" because it was believed to have started in Spain, it more likely started at U.S. Army camps in Kansas and may not have been a flu virus at all. A 2008 study by the National Institute of Allergy and Infectious Diseases suggested bacteria might have caused the pandemic.

Whatever caused it, it was devastating. Unlike normal influenza outbreaks, whose victims are generally the elderly and the young, the Spanish flu often targeted healthy young adults. By early summer, the disease had spread around the world. In New York City alone, 20,000 people died. Western Samoa lost 20 percent of its population, and entire Inuit villages in Alaska were wiped out. By the time it had run its course in 1921, the flu had killed from 25 million to 50 million people around the world. More than 500,000 Americans died, which was a greater total than all the Americans killed in all the wars of the 20th century.

26. Where did the Spanish flu begin?

    (A) Spain

    (B) army camps

    (C) New York City

    (D) Western Samoa

27. How many Americans died of the Spanish flu?

    (A) 20% of its population

    (B) more than 20,000 people

    (C) more than 500,000 people

    (D) 25 to 50 million people

Questions 28–30 are based on the following graphs.

Population by Age and Sex: 2012, 2035 and 2060

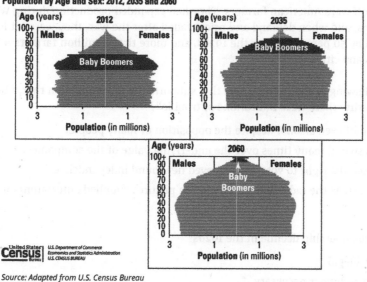

Source: Adapted from U.S. Census Bureau

28. Look at the population pyramid for the year 2012. Notice that the edges appear ragged. Shorter lines mean fewer people in that age group. There are noticeably fewer people in the 30-to-40 age group. In approximately what time period would these people have been born?

(A) 1960 to 1970

(B) 1970 to 1980

(C) 1980 to 1990

(D) 1990 to 2000

29. Which of the following reasons best explains why there are fewer people in the 30-to-40 age group in the 2012 graph?

(A) Economic troubles and the Vietnam War were going on at the time of their birth.

(B) The Korean War was going on at the time of their birth.

(C) The first Gulf War was going on at the time of their birth.

(D) The invasion of Grenada was going on at the time of their birth.

30. Look at the top of the three pyramids. Are there more men or women in the age group of 80+? ☐

Questions 31 and 32 refer to the following passage about the 1920s, excerpted from U.S. History For Dummies, *by Steve Wiegand (Wiley).*

Below the veneer of prosperity, there were indications of trouble. More and more wealth was being concentrated in fewer and fewer hands, and government did far more for the rich than the poor. It was estimated, for example, that federal tax cuts saved the hugely wealthy financier Andrew Mellon (who also happened to be Hoover's treasury secretary) almost as much money as was saved by all the taxpayers in the entire state of Nebraska.

Supreme Court decisions struck down minimum wage laws for women and children and made it easier for big business to swallow up smaller ones and become *de facto* monopolies. And union membership declined as organized labor was unable to compete with the aura of good times.

Probably worst off were American farmers. They had expanded production during World War I to feed the troops, and when demand and prices faded after the war, they were hit hard. Farm income dropped by 50 percent during the 1920s, and more than 3 million farmers left their farms for towns and cities.

31. Which of the following is another example that supports the generalization that, "Below the veneer of prosperity, there were indications of trouble"?

   (A) Prohibition outlawed alcohol despite the opposition of many people.

   (B) Stock prices soared many times over the underlying value of the companies.

   (C) Women gained the right to vote and achieved newfound independence.

   (D) Inventions such as the radio and sound motion pictures supplied entertainment to millions.

32. Why did union membership decline in the 1920s?

   (A) Unions were illegal.

   (B) Unions were no longer necessary.

   (C) Growing prosperity made unions seem less relevant.

   (D) The government did far more for the rich than for the poor.

Questions 33–35 are based on the following excerpt from The Wealth of Nations, *by Adam Smith (Thrifty Books).*

The increase of revenue and stock is the increase of national wealth. . . . Is this improvement in the circumstances of the lower ranks of the people to be regarded as an advantage or as an inconvenience to the society? The answer seems at first sight abundantly plain. Servants, laborers, and workmen of different kinds, make up the far greater part of every great political society. But what improves the circumstances of the greater part can never be regarded as an inconvenience to the whole. No society can surely be flourishing and happy, of which the far greater part of the members are poor and miserable. It is but equity, besides, that they who feed, clothe, and lodge the whole body of the people, should have such a share of the produce of their own labor as to be themselves tolerably well fed, clothed, and lodged. The liberal reward of labor, as it encourages the propagation, so it increases the industry of the common people. The wages of labor are the encouragement of industry, which, like every other human quality, improves in proportion to the encouragement it receives. A plentiful subsistence increases the bodily strength of the laborer, and the comfortable hope of bettering his condition, and of ending his days perhaps in ease and plenty, animates him to exert that strength to the utmost. Where wages are high, accordingly, we shall always find the workmen more active, diligent, and expeditious than where they are low.

33. What does Smith mean by "what improves the circumstances of the greater part can never be regarded as an inconvenience to the whole"?

   (A) Paying the working class more is an inconvenience to everyone.

   (B) Whatever improves conditions for most people cannot be regarded as bad for society as a whole.

   (C) Only circumstance that helps some improves life for all.

   (D) Company owners don't need to share profits with their employees.

34. According to Adam Smith, how should employers treat the financial well-being of their employees?

(A) Keep wages as low as possible.

(B) Reward a laborer liberally.

(C) Under no circumstances consider changes.

(D) Avoid the issue.

35. When Henry Ford's Model T car proved to be a success, he doubled his workers' wages, even when all other car manufacturers at the time would not raise wages. Would he and Adam Smith have agreed on this issue?

(A) Yes. Well-paid workers are more active and diligent.

(B) No. Paying workers more only encourages sloth.

(C) Yes. It is only fair.

(D) No. A business must remain competitive.

Answers and explanations

1. **representative.** In America, citizens elect officials, from state representatives to federal senators, who represent the interests of individual citizens in the administration of the country.

2. **A. a vote on issuing library bonds.** Choices (B), (C), and (D) are all examples of indirect or representative democracy, where someone is elected to *represent* the voter. For example, mayors, who citizens elect directly, are in office to represent them. The voters don't make political decisions; the mayor does. Only in a referendum is the voters' voice directly applied to a decision.

TIP

> This question is a good example of a common GED question type: finding an example, in this case an example of direct democracy. Answering a question such as this one requires you to show your understanding of a general concept, direct democracy, by finding an example of it.

3. **C. the former USSR.** The former USSR (Choice C), also known as the Soviet Union, was run by a government that allowed elections but with only one political party. The party, not the people, decided who would run for office. Although the form resembled democracy, it didn't allow for pluralism or political choice. The other countries are all pluralist. Canada (Choice A) is a parliamentary democracy with five major political parties. Sweden (Choice B) is also a parliamentary democracy, and like Canada, has a monarch as head of state. It, too, has several political parties contending for office in free elections. South Korea (Choice D) is a republic, run by a legislative assembly and a president elected by popular vote.

4. **A. their senator.** Of the offices in the list, only senators are elected. The others are appointed by the president.

5. **7,500 miles.** Columbus miscalculated by 7,500 miles. He thought the world was considerably smaller than it actually is.

6. **B. October 12, 1492.** The Christmas Eve date refers to his subsequent arrival at the island he called Hispaniola. The other two dates are not mentioned in the text.

7. **D. They had heard stories of the gold Columbus had found.** According to the text, they were all focused on gold. Choice (B) may be partially correct, that they were looking for adventure, but Choices (A) and (C) are not supported by the text.

8. **A. The *Santa Maria* had hit a reef and sank.** Choice (B) is incorrect at this stage of his trip, and although Choices (C) and (D) may be partially correct, they're not the best answers.

9. **Asia.** Columbus wanted to find a shorter route to Asia. He never dreamed that other continents existed.

TIP

> Questions 7 and 8 are good examples of when reading all the answer choices can help you avoid a mistake. While some of the choices are partly correct, only one of the choices in each question is the best answer.

10. **B. leftover juice after sugar was pressed out of the cane.** The text states that molasses is "the juice left over after the sugar was pressed out of the cane and crystalized." The juice pressed out of the cane still contains sugar to be extracted, so Choice (A) is incorrect. The cane isn't mixed with water (Choice C), but rather the extracted juices are. And the name *Saccharum officinarum* (Choice D) is simply the Latin name for the sugar cane plant.

WARNING

> Don't be confused when the test-makers use a fancy word like *Saccharum officinarum* in the answer choices. You may be tempted to select this answer choice because it stands out from the others. This is another time when reading and evaluating all the answer choices can help you.

11. **B. 23 years.** This problem requires some simple arithmetic. The first crop, assuming Columbus's workers planted the cane as soon as they landed, was planted in 1493. The first sugar cane was presented to the King in 1516. Subtract 1493 from 1516, and you get 23. The correct answer is 23 years.

TIP

> Don't forget that you can use the on-screen calculator on the Social Studies test when math is involved. Although this question involves simple arithmetic, you don't want a small mistake to cost you an easy additional point!

12. **1,845.** To find this number in the table, first find the row on the left that shows foreign-born individuals who entered the United States after 2010. Then find the column at the top that shows high school graduates. The cell in the table where they come together shows that 1,845 thousand is the answer.

13. **high.** The data in the table consistently shows higher educational attainment in every category for employed individuals.

REMEMBER

> The data in question 13 shows that your decision to get your GED is the right one. *Keep going!*

14. **C. The growing world population means that each woman having fewer children is offset by the fact that there are more women to have children.** Even though the number of children women are having has declined, far more women exist and are available to have children. That balances out the individual birth rate decline and results in a steady number of births.

15. **A. The king's only answer to their complaints was more repression.** The first line of the text states the answer. Choice (B) has nothing to do with the belief that the king was a tyrant. Choice (C) may be correct but also has nothing to do with the reasons the king was considered a tyrant. Choice (D) does not make sense.

16. **A. The laws were usurpations.** The colonial states felt that the king and British parliament were taking upon themselves powers to which they had no right. They certainly didn't feel that the laws were magnanimous (Choice B), or examples of justice and consanguinity (Choice C), or that the parliament was paying attention to their concerns (Choice D).

17. **A. The states viewed themselves as independent entities.** At this time, the various states considered themselves as having the same rights as independent countries loosely joined in the Confederation. Therefore, the other choices are incorrect.

18. **A. the Articles of Confederation.** The original constitution of the United States was called the *Articles of Confederation* (Choice A), not *the Constitution of the Confederation* (Choice B) or *the Declaration of Independence* (Choice C). Choice (D), the *Declaration of the Rights of Man*, is from France, not the United States.

19. **D. He had many ideas on how to fix things.** The text describes Madison as a man of many ideas about how to fix the Articles of Confederation. Choice (A) is a minor consideration, and Choices (B) and (C) are irrelevant.

20. **B. to have the ability to fund extraordinary exigencies.** Madison had seen that one of the major shortcomings of the Articles of Confederation was that the federal government depended on the states to raise money. It was the need to raise money in the face of extraordinary dangers that was a key element. Therefore, the other choices are incorrect.

21. **D. Under the Articles of Confederation, the government had only very limited powers to tax.** This information is stated directly in the passage. Therefore, the other choices are incorrect.

22. **13.** The Confederation of 1776 consisted of the original 13 colonies — Connecticut, Delaware, Georgia, Maryland, Massachusetts, New Hampshire, New Jersey, New York, North Carolina, South Carolina, Pennsylvania, Rhode Island, and Virginia. These were the first states in the union. Other states were added at later dates.

23. **C. He worked in the home of Jefferson Davis.** The most important element of the choices offered is the fact that William Jackson worked in the home of Jefferson Davis, where he had direct access to all the discussions that took place (Choice C). There's no suggestion that Jackson had any military experience (Choice A), and his direct contact with Washington, D.C., grew out of his service in Davis's home (Choice B). The fact that he was African-American (Choice D) is relevant only to the extent that he was a servant in Davis's home.

24. **A. the Underground Railroad.** Harriet Tubman is best known for her key work in the Underground Railroad. Choice (B) is a song associated with the Underground Railroad but is not mentioned in the passage. Choice (C) is a less well-known accomplishment. Though Harriet Tubman acted as a spy, Choice (D) is an accomplishment of William A. Jackson.

25. **A. the Combahee River.** This information is stated directly in the passage. *Montgomery* (Choice B) refers to the name of a military officer working with Tubman, and in any case, the city of Montgomery is in Alabama, not South Carolina. She was attacking Confederate-controlled areas, not Union areas (Choice C). Atlanta (Choice D) is in Georgia, not South Carolina.

WARNING

Did you select Choice (B)? If so, you fell into a common trap—selecting an answer choice because it was mentioned in the passage in another context. *Montgomery* in this case refers to a person, not a location. Reading the question thoroughly can help you avoid this kind of error.

26. **B. army camps.** This information is stated directly in the passage. Spain (Choice A) was erroneously named as the origin of the epidemic. The places in the other choices are mentioned in the passage as having notably high death counts, not as the disease's place of origin.

27. **C. more than 500,000 people.** This information is stated directly in the passage. The other numbers are for other parts of the world or the entire world.

28. **B. 1970 to 1980.** Subtract 30 and 40 from 2012 to get the high and low end of the range, 1970 to 1980.

29. **A. economic troubles and the Vietnam War were going on at the time of their birth.** The period of 1970 to 1980 was a time of economic difficulty and the winding down of the Vietnam War. With a controversial war, rising inflation, and worries about money, people were less likely to have children at that time. The Korean War (Choice B) had ended many years earlier, and the Gulf War (Choice C) and invasion of Grenada (Choice D) were still to come.

30. **women.** If you look at the top of the three pyramids, you can see that the right side is wider than the left. The right side reflects the number of females in the population.

31. **B. Stock prices soared many times over the underlying value of the companies.** The rapidly rising prices of stocks covered up the fact that the stocks were trading at many times the true value of the companies. This is an example of a veneer of prosperity covering up an underlying problem. The remaining choices are not related to prosperity.

32. **C. Growing prosperity made unions seem less relevant.** For most people, times appeared to be good. As long as that was the feeling, there seemed to be no real need for labor to organize. Unions were no longer illegal, so Choice (A) is incorrect. Choice (B) is contradicted by the information in the passage; the defeat of minimum wage laws showed that unions still had a role to play. Choice (D) is a reason that made unions relevant, despite people's perception of them at the time, and so is incorrect.

33. **B. Whatever improves conditions for most people cannot be regarded as bad for society as a whole.** Adam Smith proposes that anything that helps those less well off can only improve society as a whole (Choice B). The other choices are not supported by information in the passage.

34. **B. Reward a laborer liberally.** According to Smith, employers should reward their laborers generously. The other options are contradicted by the text, when Smith states, "no society can surely be flourishing and happy, of which the far greater part of the members are poor and miserable."

35. **A. Yes. Well-paid workers are more active and diligent.** Smith and Ford would have been of one mind on this issue. Ford came under attack by other wealthy industrialists for granting his workers this pay increase, but he argued that paying his workers well allowed them to buy his cars, thereby improving his own business while making the workers happy. Therefore, Choices (B) and (D) are incorrect. Choice (C) is incorrect because Ford was interested in increasing his business, not fairness.

Science Sample Questions

The Science test consists of a series of items intended to measure general concepts in science. The items are based on short readings that may include a graph, chart, or figure. Study the information given and then answer the question(s) following it. Refer to the information as often as necessary in answering the questions.

Questions

Questions 1 and 2 refer to the following diagram and excerpt adapted from NASA's Glenn Research Center website for Space Flight Systems.

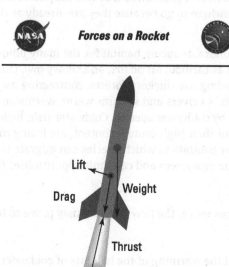

Source: NASA

Many differences exist between the forces acting on a rocket and those acting on an airplane.

- On an airplane, the **lift force** (the aerodynamic force perpendicular to the flight direction) is used to overcome the **weight**. On a rocket, **thrust** is used in opposition to weight. On many rockets, **lift** is used to stabilize and control the direction of flight.

- On an airplane, most of the aerodynamic forces are generated by the wings and the tail surfaces. For a rocket, the aerodynamic forces are generated by the fins, nose cone, and body tube. For both airplane and rocket, the aerodynamic forces act through the center of pressure (the dot with the black center on the figure), while the weight acts through the center of gravity (the solid dot on the figure).

- While most airplanes have a high lift-to-drag ratio, the drag of a rocket is usually much greater than the lift.

- While the magnitude and direction of the forces remain fairly constant for an airplane, the magnitude and direction of the forces acting on a rocket change dramatically during a typical flight.

1. In the diagram, which force must be the greatest for the rocket to leave the earth?

   (A) drag

   (B) lift

   (C) thrust

   (D) weight

2. Which statement most accurately describes lift on airplanes and rockets?

   (A) On airplanes, lift holds the airplane in the air; on some rockets, lift helps steer the rocket.

   (B) On airplanes, lift helps steer the plane; on rockets, lift holds the rocket in the air.

   (C) Rockets and planes both use lift to leave the earth.

   (D) Rockets use lift; planes use thrust.

Questions 3 and 4 refer to the following excerpt adapted from the U.S. Environmental Protection Agency's website on climate change (www.epa.gov/climatechange).

As temperatures increase, the habitat ranges of many North American species are moving northward in latitude and upward in elevation. While this means a range expansion for some species, for others it means a range reduction or a movement into less hospitable habitat or increased competition. Some species have nowhere to go because they are already at the northern or upper limit of their habitat.

For example, boreal forests are invading tundra, reducing habitat for the many unique species that depend on the tundra ecosystem such as caribou, arctic fox, and snowy owl. Other observed changes in the United States include expanding oak-hickory forests, contracting maple-beech forests, and disappearing spruce-fir forests. As rivers and streams warm, warmwater fish are expanding into areas previously inhabited by coldwater species. Coldwater fish, including several trout species valued by many people for their high protein content, are losing their habitats. As waters warm, the area of feasible, cooler habitats to which species can migrate is reduced. Range shifts disturb the current state of the ecosystem and can limit opportunities for fishing and hunting.

3. As temperatures become warmer and ranges move, the new territory may prove to be less _____ for specific species.

4. Which of the following is a consequence of the warming of the habitats of coldwater fish?

   (A) Coldwater fish migrate to new habitats.

   (B) Warmwater fish move into the habitats of coldwater fish.

   (C) Coldwater fish adjust to warmer water.

   (D) Opportunities for fishing increase.

Question 5 refers to the following excerpt from Womenshealth.gov.

"Mirror, Mirror on the wall . . . who's the thinnest one of all?" According to the National Eating Disorders Association, the average American woman is 5 feet 4 inches tall and weighs 140 pounds. The average American model is 5 feet 11 inches tall and weighs 117 pounds. All too often, society associates being "thin" with "hard-working, beautiful, strong and self-disciplined." On the other hand, being "fat" is associated with being "lazy, ugly, weak and lacking will-power." Because of these harsh critiques, rarely are women completely satisfied with their image. As a result, they often feel great anxiety and pressure to achieve and/or maintain an imaginary appearance.

Eating disorders are serious medical problems. Anorexia nervosa, bulimia nervosa, and binge-eating disorder are all types of eating disorders. Eating disorders frequently develop during adolescence or early adulthood but can occur during childhood or later in adulthood. Females are more likely than males to develop an eating disorder.

5. Which of the following would add further support to the passage?

   (A) Images of unusually thin women are pervasive in media.
   (B) Women have trouble losing weight.
   (C) Males are generally taller and weigh more.
   (D) Males are not subject to the same pressure about weight as women.

Question 6 refers to the following statement by the U.S. Surgeon General (www.surgeongeneral.gov).

We must increase our efforts to educate and encourage Americans to take responsibility for their own health. Over the past 20 years, the rates of overweight doubled in children and tripled in adolescents. Today nearly two out of every three American adults and 15 percent of American kids are overweight or obese. That's more than 9 million children — one in every seven kids — who are at increased risk of weight-related chronic diseases. These facts are astounding, but they are just the beginning of a chain reaction of dangerous health problems — many of which were once associated only with adults.

6. The percentage of children who are overweight or obese is estimated at

   (A) 9 percent.
   (B) 15 percent.
   (C) 20 percent.
   (D) 30 percent.

Question 7 refers to the following definition from the U.S. Environmental Protection Agency's climate change glossary (www.epa.gov/climatechange).

Black carbon (BC) is the most strongly light-absorbing component of particulate matter (PM), and is formed by the incomplete combustion of fossil fuels, biofuels, and biomass. It is emitted directly into the atmosphere in the form of fine particles.

7. Based on this information, why would reducing automobile use result in a cleaner environment?

   (A) Traffic would be lighter.
   (B) Most automobiles run on fossil fuel.
   (C) Subways are a more efficient form of moving people.
   (D) Electricity is less expensive than fossil fuels.

Question 8 refers to the following definition from the U.S. Environmental Protection Agency's climate change glossary (www.epa.gov/climatechange).

The greenhouse effect is the trapping and build-up of heat in the atmosphere (troposphere) near the Earth's surface. Some of the heat flowing back toward space from the Earth's surface is absorbed by water vapor, carbon dioxide, ozone, and several other gases in the atmosphere and then reradiated back toward the Earth's surface. If the atmospheric concentrations of these greenhouse gases rise, the average temperature of the lower atmosphere will gradually increase.

8. Heat reradiated from the Earth's surface is absorbed by several ⬚ in the Earth's atmosphere.

Question 9 refers to the following excerpt from NASA's Science website (science.nasa.gov).

Examples of the types of forecasts that may be possible are the outbreak and spread of harmful algal blooms, occurrence and spread of invasive exotic species, and productivity of forest and agricultural systems. This Focus Area also will contribute to the improvement of climate projections for 50–100 years into the future by providing key inputs for climate models. This includes projections of future atmospheric CO_2 and CH_4 concentrations and understanding of key ecosystem and carbon cycle process controls on the climate system.

9. Long-term forecasts of this type are important to people because

   (A) they will help hunters know when their favorite sport will become impossible.
   (B) they will allow scientists to develop research projects that will address the consequences of dramatic climate change.
   (C) people will know what type of winter clothing to buy for their children.
   (D) it will spur research into more efficient subway systems.

Question 10 refers to the following excerpt from NASA's Science website (science.nasa.gov).

Throughout the next decade, research will be needed to advance our understanding of and ability to model human-ecosystems-climate interactions so that an integrated understanding of Earth System function can be applied to our goals. These research activities will yield knowledge of the Earth's ecosystems and carbon cycle, as well as projections of carbon cycle and ecosystem responses to global environmental change.

10. This type of research should lead to advances in our understanding of how the carbon cycle and our ecosystem respond to [   ].

Questions 11 and 12 refer to the following excerpt from NASA's Jet Propulsion Laboratory website (www.jpl.nasa.gov).

We live on a restless planet. Earth is continually influenced by the Sun, gravitational forces, processes emanating from deep within the core, and by complex interactions with oceans and atmospheres. At very short time scales we seem to be standing on terra firma, yet many processes sculpt the surface with changes that can be quite dramatic (earthquakes, volcanic eruptions, landslides), sometimes slow (subsidence due to aquifer depletion), seemingly unpredictable, and often leading to loss of life and property damage.

Accurate diagnosis of our restless planet requires an observational capability for precise measurement of surface change, or deformation. Measurement of both the slow and fast deformations of Earth are essential for improving the scientific understanding of the physical processes, for optimizing responses to natural hazards, and for identifying potential risk areas.

11. Although people often talk about standing on solid ground, the truth is that

   (A) the Earth is capable of supporting huge buildings anywhere on its surface.
   (B) the ground is solid and stable.
   (C) the ground is capable of sudden, dramatic movement.
   (D) people should not live near an active volcano.

12. Accurate scientific research into surface change is essential to

(A) offset the physical processes.

(B) warn people about volcanoes.

(C) ensure better responses to natural hazards.

(D) make more accurate weather forecasts.

Question 13 refers to the following diagram from NASA's Glenn Research Center website (www.grc.nasa.gov).

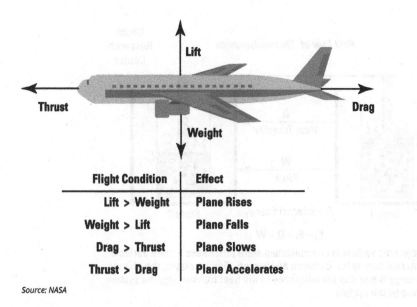

Flight Condition	Effect
Lift > Weight	Plane Rises
Weight > Lift	Plane Falls
Drag > Thrust	Plane Slows
Thrust > Drag	Plane Accelerates

Source: NASA

13. For the plane to take off, [   ] and [   ]. Write the appropriate answers in the boxes.

(A) lift > weight

(B) weight > lift

(C) drag > thrust

(D) thrust > drag

Question 14 refers to the following excerpt from NASA's website (www.nasa.gov).

It would be impractical, in terms of volume and cost, to completely stock the International Space Station (ISS) with oxygen or water for long periods of time. Without a grocery store in space, NASA scientists and engineers have developed innovative solutions to meet astronauts' basic requirements for life. The human body is two-thirds water. It has been estimated that nearly an octillion (1,000,000,000,000,000,000,000,000,000) water molecules flow through our bodies daily. It is therefore necessary for humans to consume a sufficient amount of water, as well as oxygen and food, on a daily basis in order to sustain life. Without water, the average person lives approximately three days. Without air, permanent brain damage can occur within three minutes. Scientists have determined how much water, air, and food a person needs per day per person for life on Earth. Similarly, space scientists know what is needed to sustain life in space.

14. Why is it necessary to recycle air and water on a space ship?

(A) to keep the interior smelling clean

(B) to keep the ISS moving

(C) to keep the astronauts alive

(D) so that they don't get thirsty between meals

Question 15 refers to the following diagram from NASA's Glenn Research Center website (https://www.nasa.gov/centers/glenn/home/index.html).

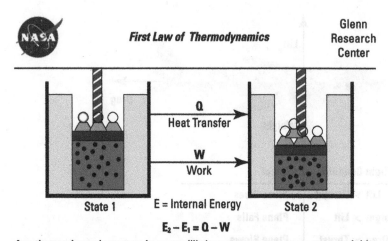

Any thermodynamic system in an equilibrium state possesses a state variable called the internal energy (E). Between any two equilibrium states, the change in internal energy is equal to the difference of the heat transfer <u>into</u> the system and work done <u>by</u> the system.

Source: NASA

15. Circle the vessel on the diagram with the higher temperature.

Questions 16 and 17 refer to the following excerpt from the Department of Agriculture website (www.usda.gov).

As the centerpiece of First Lady Michelle Obama's Let's Move! initiative to raise a healthier generation of kids, USDA led the effort to pass the Healthy, Hunger-Free Kids Act, historic legislation to allow us, for the first time in 30 years, the chance to make real reforms to the school lunch and breakfast programs by improving the critical nutrition and hunger safety net for nearly 32 million children who eat school lunch each day and the 12 million who eat breakfast at school.

The USDA's efforts to improve and enhance the school food environment include the following:

- Updated science-based school meal standards for the National School Lunch Program to increase fruits, vegetables, whole grains, and low-fat dairy while reducing fats, sodium, and sugars;

- Performance-based funding increases of 6 cents per lunch for schools meeting the new meal standards; this is the first real increase in 30 years;

- Implemented new snack-food standards in schools that preserve flexibility for time-honored traditions like fundraisers and bake sales, and provide ample transition time for schools;

- Provision of training and technical assistance to help schools meet improved standards. USDA is working closely with schools to move swiftly to make these reforms a reality in every school.

16. The Healthy, Hunger-Free Kids Act includes efforts to

    (A) increase free breakfasts.

    (B) increase the amount of sodium and sugars in school meals.

    (C) increase the amount of whole grains and vegetables in school meals.

    (D) increase the number of bake sales elementary schools can hold.

17. Which of the following is necessary for the Healthy, Hunger-Free Kids Act to succeed?

    (A) School personnel must receive training and support.

    (B) The price of school lunches must be reduced by 6 cents.

    (C) More schools must provide free snacks to students.

    (D) The number of students who are entitled to free school breakfasts should increase to 32 million.

Question 18 refers to the following definition adapted from the U.S. Environmental Protection Agency's climate change glossary (www.epa.gov/climate-change).

Weather is an atmospheric condition at any given time or place. It is measured in terms of such things as wind, temperature, humidity, atmospheric pressure, cloudiness, and precipitation. In most places, weather can change from hour-to-hour, day-to-day, and season-to-season. Climate is usually defined as the "average weather," or more rigorously, as the statistical description in terms of the mean and variability of relevant quantities over a period of time ranging from months to thousands or millions of years. The classical period is 30 years, as defined by the World Meteorological Organization (WMO). These quantities are most often surface variables such as temperature, precipitation, and wind. Climate in a wider sense is the state, including a statistical description, of the climate system. A simple way of remembering the difference is that climate is what you expect (e.g., cold winters) and weather is what you get (e.g., a blizzard).

18. If you were sitting around with a group of friends complaining about how the rain forecast for tomorrow was going to ruin your baseball game, you would be complaining about the
    [   ].

Question 19 refers to the following definition from the U.S. Environmental Protection Agency's climate change glossary (www.epa.gov/climate-change).

Atmospheric lifetime is the average time that a molecule resides in the atmosphere before it is removed by chemical reaction or deposition. This can also be thought of as the time that it takes after the human-caused emission of a gas for the concentrations of that gas in the atmosphere to return to natural levels. Greenhouse gas lifetimes can range from a few years to a few thousand years.

19. Why is it important for humans to become more aware of the pollution they are causing by overuse of fossil fuels?

    (A) Gasoline is becoming expensive.

    (B) The greenhouse gases can remain in the atmosphere for many years.

    (C) Traffic congestion is causing health problems.

    (D) Humans are turning the blue sky gray.

Question 20 refers to the following excerpt from the U.S. Department of Energy's website (www. energy.gov).

In 2009, President Barack Obama signed an Executive Order creating the White House Council on Women and Girls. In his remarks at the signing, the President underscored that the purpose of the Council is "to ensure that each of the agencies in which they're charged takes into account the needs of women and girls in the policies they draft." The Energy Department's chapter of the Council continues to pull program offices and National Laboratories together to work on confronting the challenges faced by women and girls.

At the Clean Energy Ministerial held in London in April 2012, the Department launched the U.S. Clean Energy, Education, and Empowerment (C3E) program to advance the careers and leadership of women in clean energy fields. The program, led by the Department in partnership with the MIT Energy Initiative, includes an ambassador network, annual symposium and the C3E Awards program.

A year later, inspired by the success of C3E, Energy Secretary Ernest Moniz launched the Minorities in Energy (MIE) Initiative. The initiative includes a network of more than 30 senior-level Ambassadors across the public and private sector working alongside the Department to increase the participation of minorities in energy careers as well as support their advancement to leadership positions.

20. The effect of President Obama's initiative was to ⬜ the participation of women and minorities in careers in energy-related fields.

Question 21 refers to the following excerpt from NASA's Earth Observatory website (www. earthobservatory.nasa.gov).

If Kepler's laws define the motion of the planets, Newton's laws define motion. Thinking on Kepler's laws, Newton realized that all motion, whether it was the orbit of the Moon around the Earth or an apple falling from a tree, followed the same basic principles. "To the same natural effects," he wrote, "we must, as far as possible, assign the same causes." Previous Aristotelian thinking, physicist Stephen Hawking has written, assigned different causes to different types of motion. By unifying all motion, Newton shifted the scientific perspective to a search for large, unifying patterns in nature. Newton outlined his laws in *Philosophiae Naturalis Principia Mathematica* ("Mathematical Principles of Natural Philosophy"), published in 1687.

21. Newton was inspired by

(A) Hawking.

(B) Aristotle.

(C) Kepler.

(D) Einstein.

Question 22 refers to the following information, taken from the U.S. Department of Labor's Occupational Safety & Health Administration website (www.osha.gov).

Unexpected releases of toxic, reactive, or flammable liquids and gases in processes involving highly hazardous chemicals have been reported for many years. Incidents continue to occur in various industries that use highly hazardous chemicals which may be toxic, reactive, flammable, or explosive, or may exhibit a combination of these properties. Regardless of the industry that uses these highly hazardous chemicals, there is a potential for an accidental release any time they are not properly controlled. This, in turn, creates the possibility of disaster.

Recent major disasters include the 1984 Bhopal, India, incident resulting in more than 2,000 deaths; the October 1989 Phillips Petroleum Company, Pasadena, TX, incident resulting in 23 deaths and 132 injuries; the July 1990 BASF, Cincinnati, OH, incident resulting in 2 deaths, and the May 1991 IMC, Sterlington, LA, incident resulting in 8 deaths and 128 injuries.

22. Of the incidents reported in the passage, which one caused the most fatalities?

(A) Bhopal, India

(B) Pasadena, Texas

(C) Cincinnati, Ohio

(D) Sterlington, Louisiana

Question 23 is based on the following excerpt from the National Oceanic and Atmospheric Administration's Office of Response and Restoration website (response.restoration.noaa.gov).

Reactivity is the tendency of substances to undergo chemical change, which can result in hazards — such as heat generation or toxic gas by-products. The CRW (Chemical Reactivity Worksheet) predicts possible hazards from mixing chemicals and is designed to be used by emergency responders and planners, as well as the chemical industry, to help prevent dangerous chemical incidents.

The chemical datasheets in the CRW database contain information about the intrinsic hazards of each chemical and about whether a chemical reacts with air, water, or other materials. It also includes case histories on specific chemical incidents, with references.

23. What is the most important contribution of the CRW to the prevention of hazardous accidents?

(A) provides information

(B) enforces the regulations

(C) creates laws

(D) closes companies for infractions

Question 24 refers to the following excerpt from the U.S. Environmental Protection Agency's website on climate change (www.epa.gov/climate-change).

Climate change, along with habitat destruction and pollution, is one of the important stressors that can contribute to species extinction. The IPCC estimates that 20–30% of the plant and animal species evaluated so far in climate change studies are at risk of extinction if temperatures reach levels projected to occur by the end of this century. Projected rates of species extinctions are 10 times greater than recently observed global average rates and 10,000 times greater than rates observed in the distant past (as recorded in fossils).

24. One of the great dangers to the earth as a result of climate change is the [ ] of species.

Question 25 refers to the following excerpt from the U.S. Environmental Protection Agency's website on climate change (www.epa.gov/climate-change).

When coral reefs become stressed, they expel microorganisms that live within their tissues and are essential to their health. This is known as coral bleaching. As ocean temperatures warm and the acidity of the ocean increases, bleaching and coral die-offs are likely to become more frequent. Chronically stressed coral reefs are less likely to recover.

25. Coral bleaching refers to

(A) a chemical reaction between the ocean waters and microorganisms in the coral.

(B) expulsion of microorganisms from within coral reefs.

(C) the effect of extremely strong sunlight on coral reefs.

(D) coral die-offs.

Question 26 refers to the following excerpt from the U.S. Environmental Protection Agency's website on climate change (www.epa.gov/climate-change).

For many species, the climate where they live or spend part of the year influences key stages of their annual life cycle, such as migration, blooming, and mating. As the climate has warmed in recent decades, the timing of these events has changed in some parts of the country. Some examples are

- Warmer springs have led to earlier nesting for 28 migratory bird species on the East Coast of the United States.

- Northeastern birds that winter in the southern United States are returning north in the spring 13 days earlier than they did in the early 20th century.

- In a California study, 16 out of 23 butterfly species shifted their migration timing and arrived earlier.

Changes like these can lead to mismatches in the timing of migration, breeding, and food availability. Growth and survival are reduced when migrants arrive at a location before or after food sources are present.

26. The information in the passage implies that a rise in Arctic temperature may result in

(A) an increase in the nutrient-rich pockets in the ice.

(B) a decline in the number of polar bears.

(C) an extension of the sea ice.

(D) an increase in the species of zooplankton.

Question 27 refers to the following excerpt from the U.S. Environmental Protection Agency's stratospheric ozone glossary (www.epa.gov/ozone-layer-protection).

Consumer aerosol products in the United States have not used ozone-depleting substances (ODS) since the late 1970s because of voluntary switching followed by federal regulation. The Clean Air Act and EPA regulations further restricted the use of ODS for non-consumer products. All consumer products, and most other aerosol products, now use propellants that do not deplete the ozone layer, such as hydrocarbons and compressed gases.

27. The propellants that are currently used in aerosol products are [_____] and [_____].

Question 28 refers to the following definition from the U.S. Environmental Protection Agency's climate change glossary (www.epa.gov/climate-change).

Biofuels are gas or liquid fuels made from plant material (biomass). They include wood, wood waste, wood liquors, peat, railroad ties, wood sludge, spent sulfite liquors, agricultural waste, straw, tires, fish oils, tall oil, sludge waste, waste alcohol, municipal solid waste, landfill gases, other waste, and ethanol blended into motor gasoline.

28. Biofuels are ecologically sound because

    (A) they are inexpensive

    (B) they do not pollute the Earth

    (C) they are made from indestructible materials

    (D) they can be used as fuels

Question 29 refers to the following definition from the U.S. Environmental Protection Agency's climate change glossary (www.epa.gov/climate-change).

The carbon cycle is all parts (reservoirs) and fluxes of carbon. The cycle is usually thought of as four main reservoirs of carbon interconnected by pathways of exchange. The reservoirs are the atmosphere, terrestrial biosphere (usually includes freshwater systems), oceans, and sediments (includes fossil fuels). The annual movements of carbon, the carbon exchanges between reservoirs, occur because of various chemical, physical, geological, and biological processes. The ocean contains the largest pool of carbon near the surface of the Earth, but most of that pool is not involved with rapid exchange with the atmosphere.

29. The largest pool of carbon on Earth is the [   ].

Questions 30 and 31 refer to the following definition from the U.S. Environmental Protection Agency's climate change glossary (www.epa.gov/climate-change).

Carbon footprint is the total amount of greenhouse gases that are emitted into the atmosphere each year by a person, family, building, organization, or company. A person's carbon footprint includes greenhouse gas emissions from fuel that an individual burns directly, such as by heating a home or riding in a car. It also includes greenhouse gases that come from producing the goods or services that the individual uses, including emissions from power plants that make electricity, factories that make products, and landfills where trash gets sent.

30. Which of the following would increase people's individual carbon footprint?

    (A) walking more and driving less

    (B) lowering their thermostats during the cold weather

    (C) not barbequing

    (D) taking airplanes more frequently

31. People's personal carbon footprints are also affected by processes out of their control, such as

    (A) grocery shopping.

    (B) recycling depots.

    (C) power plants.

    (D) driving less.

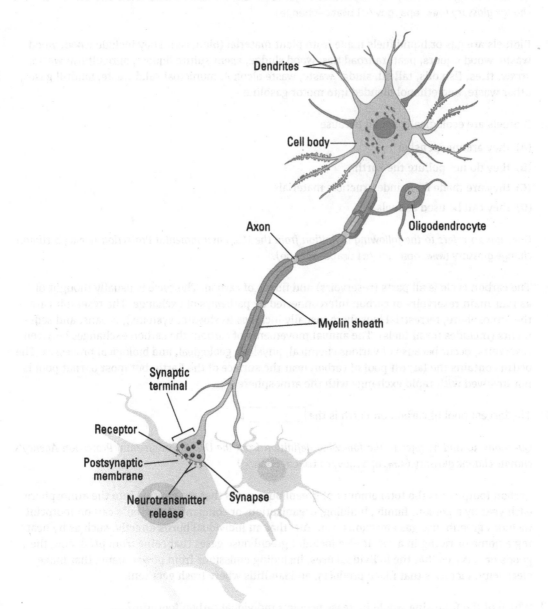

Dendrites

Cell body

Axon

Oligodendrocyte

Myelin sheath

Synaptic terminal

Receptor

Postsynaptic membrane

Neurotransmitter release

Synapse

Source: U.S. Department of Health and Human Services

32. The nerve cells in your body carry messages in the form of electrical signals. The signals travel from the cell body along the axon, which is protected by the _____.

Question 33 refers to the following excerpt from NASA's website (www.nasa.gov).

Saving lives does not have to be as complex as robotic surgery but can be as simple as providing the life-giving source of clean water. This specifically is of utmost importance to a community in rural Mexico, showing the far-reaching benefits of the water purification component of NASA's Environmental and Life Control Support System (ECLSS). ECLSS provides clean water for drinking, cooking and hygiene aboard the space station. This technology has been adapted on Earth to aid remote locations or places devastated by natural disaster that do not have access to clean drinking water.

In Chiapas, Mexico, many people are at risk of illness from drinking contaminated water from wells, rivers or springs not treated by municipal water systems. Children in Chiapas, previously sickened by parasites and stomach bugs, now have access during school to clean, safe drinking water. This is due to the installation of the ECLSS-derived water purification plant. Renewable solar energy powers the water treatment technology for the community in Chiapas. Results include improved overall health and cost-savings from not having to buy purified water or medication to treat water-borne illnesses.

33. How do innovations by NASA help a little town in Mexico?

   (A) by setting up space industries

   (B) by providing for clean water

   (C) by supplying food

   (D) by ridding the area of parasites

Question 34 refers to the following excerpt from the U.S. Department of Labor's Occupational Safety & Health Administration website (www.osha.gov).

Chemicals have the ability to react when exposed to other chemicals or certain physical conditions. The reactive properties of chemicals vary widely, and they play a vital role in the production of many chemical, material, pharmaceutical, and food products we use daily. When chemical reactions are not properly managed, they can have harmful, or even catastrophic consequences, such as toxic fumes, fires, and explosions. These reactions may result in death and injury to people, damage to physical property, and severe effects on the environment.

34. What is the main idea of this passage?

   (A) Chemicals can poison the food supply.

   (B) Chemicals can have dire consequences if not handled properly.

   (C) Chemicals play a vital role in our lives.

   (D) Chemicals have many advantages, but also pose serious risks.

Question 35 refers to the following chart.

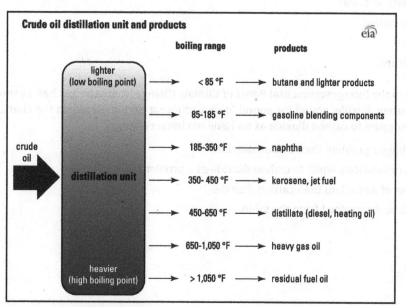

Source: U.S. Energy Information Administration

35. Why is it easier to obtain naphtha from crude oil in a distillation unit than diesel oil?

(A) It naturally floats to the surface where it can be skimmed off.

(B) It has a lower boiling point, so it evaporates sooner than diesel oil.

(C) It has a higher boiling point, so it remains behind as diesel is evaporated.

(D) Naphtha can be filtered out.

Questions 36 and 37 refer to the following chart.

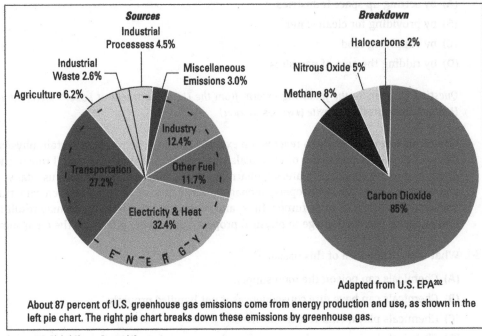

About 87 percent of U.S. greenhouse gas emissions come from energy production and use, as shown in the left pie chart. The right pie chart breaks down these emissions by greenhouse gas.

Source: U.S. Global Change Research Program

36. What is the largest single source of greenhouse gas emissions in the United States?

(A) electricity and heat

(B) transportation

(C) industry

(D) agriculture

37. According to the Intergovernmental Panel of Climate Change, methane gas has 34 times the effect of carbon dioxide, pound for pound, over a 100-year period. Based on the chart, how does methane compare to carbon dioxide as an issue in climate change?

(A) It is a bigger problem than carbon dioxide.

(B) It is approximately equal to carbon dioxide as a problem.

(C) It is less of a problem than carbon dioxide.

(D) Cannot be determined from the table.

Questions 38 to 39 refer to the following diagram.

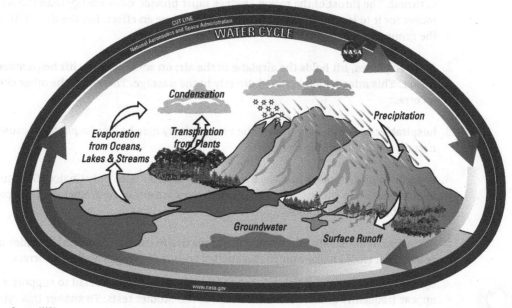

Source: NASA

38. What is the energy source that powers the water cycle?

(A) wind

(B) solar energy

(C) geothermal energy

(D) hydroelectric power

39. How does surface runoff of water eventually return to the atmosphere?

(A) It collects in lakes and streams and evaporates.

(B) It is absorbed into the ground.

(C) It is used by plants to make food.

(D) It falls as precipitation.

40. Based on the diagram of the water cycle, the purest water would be found in which of the following?

(A) the rivers

(B) the groundwater

(C) the ocean

(D) the mountain ice caps

Answers and explanations

1. **C. thrust.** The thrust of the rocket engines must provide more energy than the weight of the rocket for it to leave the earth. The other forces have an effect, but the thrust lifts it off the ground.

2. **A. On airplanes, lift holds the airplane in the air; on some rockets, lift helps steer the rocket.** This information is stated directly in the passage. Therefore, the other choices are incorrect.

3. **hospitable.** As the passage states, the new territory may be less *hospitable* because of the natural conditions of the territory.

4. **B. warmwater fish move into the habitats of coldwater fish.** Only Choice (B) is supported by information in the passage. The other choices are either contradicted by the passage or cannot be concluded from it.

5. **A. Images of unusually thin women are pervasive in media.** Choice (A) provides another reason that would make women dissatisfied with their images and so is correct.

   Questions of this type, which ask you to identify an additional detail to support a main idea, appear frequently on the GED Science and Social Studies tests. To answer this type of item, identify the main idea in the passage. Then find the answer choice that most effectively supports that main idea.

6. **B. 15 percent.** The passage clearly states, "15 percent of American kids are overweight or obese."

   This question is a good example of when reading the question first can help you find the answer. In this case, you can look for the specific number, 15, as you read the passage.

7. **B. Most automobiles run on fossil fuel.** Most automobiles run on gasoline, which is a fossil fuel, the incomplete combustion of which forms black carbon. The other choices may be important from a traffic congestion or economic point of view but aren't mentioned in the passage and do not answer the question.

8. **gases.** The passage states that water vapor, carbon dioxide, ozone, and several other gases are responsible for the reradiation of heat from the Earth's surface.

9. **B. they will allow scientists to develop research projects that will address the consequences of dramatic climate change.** More accurate forecasts will allow scientists to work on experiments to address the changes that may be coming. Choices (A) and (C) may be possibilities but aren't mentioned in the passage. Choice (D) is probably a good general idea but has nothing to do with the passage.

10. **global environmental change.** The passage states this as one of the results of this research.

11. **C. the ground is capable of sudden, dramatic movement.** Some of the examples given to support this choice are volcanic eruptions, earthquakes, and landslides. The other choices aren't supported by any content in the passage, although Choice (D) is probably a good idea.

12. **C. ensure better responses to natural hazards.** The other choices aren't mentioned in the passage.

13. **A. lift > weight; D. thrust > drag.** For a plane to take off, it must accelerate and rise. In order to do that, lift must be greater than weight and thrust must be greater than drag.

14. **C. to keep the astronauts alive.** Without a constant supply of air and water, the astronauts couldn't survive in space, and because carrying a sufficient supply of air and water would be impossible given weight restrictions, they must be recycled.

15. **State 1.** State 1 should be circled because it has the higher temperature. According to the diagram, the heat transfer, Q, would be from State 1 to State 2, indicated by the arrow labeled Q.

16. **C. increase the amount of whole grains and vegetables in school meals.** The passage states that new school meal standards for the National School Lunch Program aim to increase fruits, vegetables, whole grains, and low-fat dairy while reducing fats, sodium, and sugars.

17. **A. School personnel must receive training and support.** One of the provisions of the Act is training and technical assistance to help schools meet improved standards.

18. **weather.** *Weather* is current and is a short-term condition. *Climate* is the average weather over a period of time. So *weather* refers to the condition on any given day.

19. **B. The greenhouse gases can remain in the atmosphere for many years.** The passage states that the lifetime of greenhouse gases ranges from a few years to a few thousand years, and these gases are a danger to people's health. Choice (A) is a *truism* (a commonly heard true statement), and Choice (C) may be true but not in the context of the passage. Choice (D) may be a symptom of the increase in pollution but isn't the best choice.

20. **increase.** President Obama's initiative was aimed at increasing the participation of the two groups in science-related careers.

21. **C. Kepler.** The passage is very clear about Kepler's influence on Newton. Hawking and Einstein both lived after Newton's publication, and Aristotle differed from Newton's conclusion.

22. **A. Bhopal, India.** According to the passage, this incident resulted in more than 2,000 fatalities, which is larger than the number of fatalities at the other locations. Note that this question is a good illustration of how reading the question first can help you save time. To answer this question, you do not need to read the entire passage. You only have to find the largest number.

TIP

This question is another good example of when reading the question first can help you find the answer quickly. In this case, you can look for the location with the largest number, 2,000, as you read the passage. When you return to the question after reading, you can immediately select Bhopal and move on to the next item.

23. **A. provides information.** The CRW provides information about hazardous materials so that companies can use them safely. The other choices are incorrect according to the passage.

24. **extinction.** The passage states that climate change will cause species to become extinct at an accelerated rate.

25. **B. expulsion of microorganisms from within coral reefs.** Stressed coral reefs expel microorganisms essential to their health. Choice (A) sounds correct if you skim the passage, but it's incorrect. Choice (C) is also wrong because there's no mention of the effect of sunlight on the reefs, and Choice (D) does not make sense.

26. **B. a decline in the number of polar bears.** The passage explains the ripple effect of a food web: It can be reasonably inferred that a rise in Arctic temperature will cause a decline in the extent of sea ice, which will lead to fewer ice algae. Fewer ice algae will lead to fewer zooplankton, which will lead to fewer cod, which will lead to fewer seals. Without a sufficient diet of seals, polar bear populations will decline.

27. **hydrocarbons; compressed gases.** These two propellants are used because they don't deplete the ozone.

28. **B. they do not pollute the Earth.** Materials made from biomass tend to be made from recycled materials, making them less polluting.

29. **ocean.** Although you may not usually think of water as containing carbon, the ocean is the largest pool of carbon on Earth because the ocean isn't pure water.

30. **D. taking airplanes more frequently.** Only this action would increase people's carbon footprint. Walking more and driving your car less, lowering your thermostat during the cold weather, and not barbequing all would reduce people's carbon footprint.

31. **C. power plants.** Power plants may increase or decrease pollution depending on the process used, which tends to affect your carbon footprint positively or negatively.

32. **myelin sheath.** You can see in the diagram that the axon is surrounded by the myelin sheath, a protective coating.

33. **B. by providing for clean water.** NASA used a form of its water purification process to provide the village with clean water.

34. **D. Chemicals have many advantages, but also pose serious risks.** The passage gives the advantages and dangers of chemicals, so this choice sums up the passage best. The other choices are either advantages or disadvantages.

35. **B. It has a lower boiling point, so it evaporates sooner than diesel oil.** Naphtha is a component of crude oil. It has a lower boiling point than diesel fuel and thus evaporates at a lower temperature than diesel fuel. This allows it to be separated from the crude oil before diesel fuel.

36. **A. electricity and heat.** The production of energy and heating in the United States produces more greenhouse gases than any other single activity.

37. **D. Cannot be determined from the table.** The key term here is *by weight*. The pie chart doesn't indicate whether the emissions are by weight or by volume. Therefore, it's impossible to calculate a comparative value.

38. **B. solar energy.** The basic source that drives the water cycle on Earth is solar energy. Heat from the Sun causes water to evaporate. Heat from the Sun causes movement of air mass on Earth, thus creating winds and evaporation. Winds carry the evaporated moisture from place to place on Earth. Eventually, the evaporated moisture condenses, forming rain or other forms of precipitation.

39. **A. It collects in lakes and streams and evaporates.** Of the choices, only this one results in water returning to the atmosphere.

40. **D. the mountain ice caps.** The purest water would be found in the ice caps of the mountains because it would be the least contaminated. Water in surface runoff picks up minerals from the soil as it runs down the mountains and flows into groundwater, rivers, and oceans.

Mathematical Reasoning Sample Questions

The following math practice questions test your knowledge of mathematical operations and reading skills in math. Read the questions carefully, making sure that you understand what's being asked. You may have to convert some units of measurement to another, but in all cases, they'll make sense.

Questions

1. Vlad is shopping for new shirts because all the stores are having end-of-season sales. Sam's Shirts offers Vlad 20% off all his purchases, while Harry's Haberdashery has a special sale offering five shirts for the price of four. Tim & Tim's Clothes offers buy four, get one free. The regular price for shirts is the same at all three stores. Vlad decides to get 5 shirts. Which is the better deal?

   (A) Tim & Tim's Clothes

   (B) Sam's Shirts

   (C) Harry's Haberdashery

   (D) They are all the same.

2. Olga designed a company logo consisting of an equilateral triangle in a circle. She designed the logo with one vertex of the triangle pointing northeast. The client said she liked the design but preferred that the vertex of the triangle point due south. What rotation would Olga have to perform to satisfy her client?

   (A) 90 degrees to the right

   (B) 110 degrees to the right

   (C) 135 degrees to the left

   (D) 135 degrees to the right

3. Solve the following equation for x:

   $x = 2y + 6z - y^2$, if $y = 6$ and $z = 2$

   (A) 12

   (B) 11

   (C) −11

   (D) −12

Question 4 refers to the following table of prices for new vacuum cleaners.

Make and Model	Price
Hopper Model A1	$249.99
Vacuous Vacuum Company Model ZZ3	$679.99
Clean-R-Up Special Series	$179.00
Electrified Home Upright	$749.99
Super Suction 101	$568.99

4. Nate is looking for a new vacuum cleaner for his apartment. He has been told by his best friend that spending around the average price will get him an adequate unit. Which vacuum cleaner is closest to the average price for vacuum cleaners? ╰──────────╯

5. Evaluate the following formula:

$N = a + c - 2ac$, if $a = 5$ and $c = 3$

(A) -22

(B) 22

(C) 28

(D) 38

6. Solve the following equation for x. $3x + 12 = 24$

(A) 3

(B) 4

(C) 5

(D) 12

7. Rachel and Ronda were planning for their first apartment, and they decided to split the required shopping tasks. Rachel was responsible for finding out how much it would cost to carpet their living room, and Ronda was responsible for finding out how much it would cost to paint the bedroom walls. What formula would each of them need to use to get an answer that would let them figure out the price for each job?

(A) $P = 2(l + w)$

(B) $A = l \times w$

(C) $V = l \times w \times d$

(D) $A = \pi r^2$

8. Lillian is drawing a scale diagram of her apartment to take with her while shopping for rugs. If she has taken all the measurements in the apartment, what mathematical relationship would she use to draw the scale drawing?

(A) decimals

(B) exponents

(C) ratios

(D) addition

9. Sylvia couldn't fall asleep one night and got to wondering how much water her bedroom would hold if she filled it to the ceiling. She had previously measured all the walls and knew all the measurements, including length, width, and height. She should use _____ to calculate how many cubic feet of water would be needed to fill the room.

(A) addition

(B) subtraction

(C) multiplication

(D) division

10. Alvin is drawing a diagram of his room. He has drawn the line representing the floor and is ready to draw the line representing the wall. This line would be _____ to the line representing the floor.

  (A) congruent

  (B) parallel

  (C) similar

  (D) perpendicular

11. Aaron wants to paint the floor of his apartment. His living room/dining room is 19 feet by 16 feet, his bedroom is 12 feet by 14 feet, and his hallways are 6 feet by 8 feet. Bowing to pressure from his friends, he has decided not to paint the floor of the kitchen or the bathroom. How many square feet of floor must he paint?

  (A) 520

  (B) 304

  (C) 250

  (D) 216

Question 12 refers to the following table.

Week	Calories Consumed Per Week	Weight (Pounds)	Height (Feet/Inches)
1	12,250	125	5 ft. 1.5 in.
2	15,375	128	5 ft. 1.5 in.
3	13,485	128	5 ft. 1.5 in.
4	16,580	130	5 ft. 1.5 in.
5	15,285	129	5 ft. 1.5 in.

12. Alan kept track of his caloric intake, his weight, and his height for a period of five weeks. What conclusion can you draw from his observations?

  (A) Eating a lot makes you taller.

  (B) Eating more calories will make you gain weight.

  (C) Gaining weight will make you taller.

  (D) There's no correlation between the data presented.

13. On Monday, Mary walked 12 blocks. On Tuesday, she walked 10 blocks, and on Wednesday, she walked 14 blocks. If she wants to walk more than her average trip for those three days on Thursday, at least how many blocks must she walk?

  (A) 9

  (B) 10

  (C) 11

  (D) 13

14. Hassan has developed a new trick to play on his classmates. He asks them to write down their ages and multiply by 4, divide by 2, then subtract 6, and, finally, add 8. When they tell him the resulting number, Hassan can always tell them their age. If one of his friends tells Hassan the resultant number is 52, how old is he?

(A) 24

(B) 25

(C) 33

(D) 52

Question 15 refers to the following table.

a	b	F
1	2	–16
2	1	–3
3	2	–18
2	3	–35
3	4	x

15. Herman developed the following function to amuse himself: $F = 2a + 3b^2 - 2ab$. He kept track of his results in this table.

Using Herman's function, what is the value of x?

(A) –82

(B) 30

(C) 53

(D) 88

16. Calvin and Kelvin, carpenters extraordinaire, are building an attic staircase for their client, Ms. Coleman. The stairway is to bridge a space 10 feet high, and the distance from the front of the bottom step to the back of the top step is 14 feet. What is the slope of the attic staircase to 2 decimal places?

(A) 0.69

(B) 0.70

(C) 0.71

(D) 0.72

Questions 17 and 18 refer to the following information.

April is considering two apartments. They are of equal size except for the bedrooms. Bedroom A is 19 feet by 14 feet, and bedroom B is 17 feet by 16 feet.

17. How many square feet larger is the larger bedroom?

(A) 8

(B) 7

(C) 6

(D) 5

18. April wants an area rug for the larger bedroom that would cover the floor, leaving a space 1 foot from each wall. If the rug had a 1-inch fringe all the way around it, how many feet long would the fringe be?

(A) 85

(B) 58

(C) 55

(D) 29

19. The school nurse made this table, which shows the results he got from asking several students about their heights and birth months.

Month of Birth	Height
March	5 ft. 4 in.
June	5 ft. 6 in.
March	5 ft. 1 in.
January	5 ft. 8 in.
August	5 ft. 5 in.
January	5 ft. 6 in.

In which month was the shortest person born?

(A) January

(B) March

(C) June

(D) August

20. Order these numbers from smallest (1) to largest (4).

$\sqrt{4}$ 0.75   1/3 1^3

21. Susie is shopping for a few groceries. She buys a loaf of bread for $1.29 and a half gallon of milk on sale for $1.47. She sees her favorite cheese on sale for $2.07. If she has $5.00 in her purse, she **can / cannot** (circle one) buy the cheese if there is no tax on food.

Question 22 refers to the following table.

Annual Sales of the Wonderful World of Widgets

Year	Annual Sales (In Million Units)
2021	43
2020	29
2019	72
2018	70
2017	71

22. The general manager of the Wonderful World of Widgets wants to present these figures in a visual, easily understood way to the board of directors to help them understand the effect that the downturn in the economy in 2020 had on the sales of widgets. What would be the best way to present the figures?

(A) a graph

(B) a series of tables

(C) verbal descriptions

(D) a movie of how widgets are used in America

23. Mark the points $(3, 1)$, $(-4, -3)$, and $(-5, 5)$ on the graph to draw a geometric figure and identify the figure [＿＿＿＿].

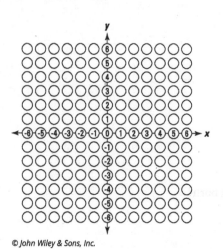

© John Wiley & Sons, Inc.

24. Georgio leaned a 25-foot ladder on the side of his house. The bottom of the ladder is 7 feet from the wall. Therefore, the top of the ladder is touching a point [＿＿＿＿] feet above the ground. You may use numbers, a decimal point (.), and/or a negative sign (−) in your answer.

25. Where are all the points with an x-coordinate of −4 located on a graph?

(A) 4 units above the x-axis

(B) 4 units below the x-axis

(C) 4 units to the right of the y-axis

(D) 4 units to the left of the y-axis

26. In a recent 10-year period, the average age of Americans claiming Social Security went up from 63.6 to 64.7 for men, and from 63.6 to 64.6 for women. How much was the age increase for women claiming Social Security over that period?

(A) 0 years

(B) 0.1 year

(C) 1 year

(D) 1.1 years

27. The students in a math class are looking at the equation $A = l \times w$. The teacher asks what result doubling the length (*l*) would have on the area (*A*). What answer is correct?

(A) makes it two times larger

(B) makes it three times larger

(C) makes it four times larger

(D) makes it five times larger

28. Herman is going to paint a wall that is 20 feet long and 8 feet high. If all of it is to be covered with one coat of primer, how many square feet of wall have to be covered with primer?

(A) 28

(B) 56

(C) 160

(D) 610

29. Where on a graph would the point $(-4, -4)$ be?

(A) four units to the right and four units below the corresponding axis

(B) four units to the left and four units below the corresponding axis

(C) four units to the left and four units above the corresponding axis

(D) four units to the right and four units above the corresponding axis

30. Roger and Ekua went shopping together. Ekua spent twice as much for clothing as Roger did. If their total expenditure for clothing was $90.00, how much did Roger spend for clothing?
$ [   ]

Answers and explanations

1. **D. They are all the same.** In this case, all the offers are for 20% off. They are just expressed differently. "Five shirts for the price of four" and "buy four and get one free" are the same deal expressed differently. Consider buying four shirts for $10 each and getting one more free. Five shirts would cost $40, or an average price of $8 each, which is 20% off the regular price ($10). Keep in mind that the same prices are often stated in different ways.

2. **D. 135 degrees to the right.** If you visualize the equilateral triangle drawn within the circle with one vertex pointing northeast, you can see that the vertex is 45 degrees above the horizontal, which is due east. Due south would be at the halfway point of the circle or at 180 degrees. Simply subtract 45 degrees (the initial position) from 180 degrees (the final position) to discover that the vertex has traveled 135 degrees to the right. Another way to answer this question is with addition. To go from due east to due south requires a rotation of 90 degrees to the right. The entire rotation would consist of 45 degrees + 90 degrees = 135 degrees to the right. If reading about this problem is confusing, draw it. Diagrams often make problems easier to visualize.

3. **D. −12.** You can solve this equation by substituting 6 for *y* and 2 for *z*, which produces this equation: $2(6) + 6(2) - 6^2 = -12$.

4. **Super Suction 101.** You can calculate the average price by adding all the prices and dividing the sum by the number of prices. To simplify the calculations, you can round to the nearest dollar. ($250 + $680 + $179 + $750 + $569) / 5 = $485.60. The machine that comes closest is the Super Suction 101 because the difference between the price of the Super Suction 101 and the average price is $569 − $486 = $83. The difference between the price of the Hopper Model A1 and the average price is $486 − $250 = $236, leaving the Super Suction 101 the clear selection, using the friend's criteria.

TIP

Note that this question is a clear example of the advantage of using rounding to make a question fast and easy to solve. That can help you keep moving from item to item on test day!

5. **A. −22.** Only this result follows the correct order of operations.

TIP

Always remember to follow the correct order of operations, which is Parentheses, Exponents, Multiplication and Division, and Addition and Subtraction. You always work from left to right, and always work multiplication and division together and addition and subtraction together. A good way to remember is with the letters PEMDAS.

6. **B. 4.** If $3x + 12 = 24$, you can subtract 12 from both sides so that $3x = 24 − 12$, or $3x = 12$; then divide both sides by 3 to find x, or $x = 4$. Again, remember the cardinal rule of equations: Whatever you do to one side, you must do to the other.

REMEMBER

As you prepare for the Mathematical Reasoning section of the GED test, you definitely want to remember this rule about equations: Whatever you do to one side of the equation, you must do to the other side.

7. **B. $A = l \times w$.** In each case, Rachel and Ronda have to calculate the area of the space they're dealing with to get a price for the carpet and the paint. The formula for area is $A = l \times w$.

8. **C. ratios.** A scale drawing involves representing one dimension with a smaller one, while keeping the shape of the room the same. Lillian may have decided to represent 1 foot in real life by 1 inch on her drawing (a ratio of 1 foot to 1 inch), resulting in a 12-foot wall being represented by a 12-inch line. None of the other three choices are mathematical relationships and would, therefore, have to be excluded immediately.

9. **C. multiplication.** The formula to calculate the volume of a room is to multiply the length by the width by the height. (On the GED test, the formula for calculating volume is listed on the formula sheet.)

10. **D. perpendicular.** The line is perpendicular because walls are perpendicular to floors. (If they weren't perpendicular, the room would probably collapse.)

11. **A. 520.** To find the total area, you must multiply the length by the width for each area. The area of the living room/dining room is $19 \times 16 = 304$ square feet, the area of the bedroom is $12 \times 14 = 168$ square feet, and the area of the hallway is $6 \times 8 = 48$ square feet. The total area is the sum of the room areas or $304 + 168 + 48 = 520$ square feet.

12. **B. Eating more calories will make you gain weight.** The more Alan ate, the heavier he became (which represents a possible causal relationship). The table provides no basis for the other answers.

If two values change in tune with each other, they have a *correlating* relationship. For example, there's a positive correlation between height and age during the teenage years. In other words, you get taller as you get older. If one event leads to another or causes another, the events form a *causal* relationship. For example, eating all the red jellybeans alters the percentage of orange jellybeans in a mixture of equal numbers of different colors because eating a red jellybean removes it from the pool of jellybeans. As a result, the percentage of orange jellybeans (and of every other remaining color) increases.

13. **D. 13.** Mary's average trip for those three days was $(12+10+14)/3 = 36/3 = 12$ blocks. To beat her average, she has to walk 13 blocks on Thursday. If she walks 12 blocks, she will equal (not beat) her average trip. All the other answers are less than her average.

14. **B. 25.** Hassan knows that multiplication and division are opposite operations, which means that multiplying by 4 and dividing by 2 produces a number twice the original. Addition and subtraction are opposites, too, so subtracting 6 and adding 8 results in a number 2 larger than the original. If the number Hassan's friend tells him is 52, Hassan simply has to subtract 2 from the resultant number (52) and divide by 2, giving him an answer of 25. Or Hassan could start with 52 and then work backward (first subtracting 8, then adding 6, and so on) through the directions to arrive at the correct answer.

15. **B. 30.** Using Herman's function, $x = 2(3) + 3(4)(4) - 2(3)(4) = 6 + 48 - 24 = 30$.

16. **C. 0.71.** To calculate the slope, you have to divide the rise by the run. That is $\frac{10}{14} = 0.7142857$, or 0.71 rounded to 2 decimal places.

The *slope* of a line is rise over run. Thus, the slope of a stairway is equal to the distance above the floor of the last step over the distance from the front of the first step to the back of the top step.

17. **C. 6.** The area of bedroom A is $19 \times 14 = 266$ square feet. The area of bedroom B is $17 \times 16 = 272$ square feet. Bedroom B is larger by $272 - 266 = 6$ square feet.

18. **B. 58.** The measure of the fringe is the perimeter of the rug. Because the rug would cover the floor 1 foot in from each wall, the length of the rug would be $17 - 2 = 15$ feet, and the width would be $16 - 2 = 14$ feet. The reason you have to subtract 2 from each measurement is that the rug would be 1 foot from each wall, resulting in a rug that was 2 feet shorter than the room in each dimension. Perimeter $= 2(l + w)$, where l is the length and w is the width, so the perimeter of the rug is $2(15 + 14) = 2(29) = 58$ feet.

19. **B. March.** The shortest person in the survey is 5 ft. 1 in. tall. That person was born in March.

20. **The correct order is (1) 1/3, (2) 0.75, (3) 1³, and (4) √4.** The largest number is $\sqrt{4}$, which is equal to 2. The exponent 1^3 is equal to 1 ($1 \times 1 \times 1 = 1$). And the fraction 1/3 (0.33) is smaller than 0.75.

21. **can.** The simplest way to solve this problem is to add the cost of the bread and milk to get $2.76, and then add the price of the cheese ($2.07) to get a total of $4.83, which is less than $5.00. You can also estimate the result by rounding and adding $1.30 and $1.50 to get $2.80, and then adding $2.10 for the cheese for a total of $4.90, which is less than $5.00. Using rounding can help you answer some questions quickly and move on to the next ones.

22. **A. a graph.** A graph is a visual representation of data; it's easily understood and can be used to compare data visually. You could use some of the other choices to represent the data, but they would all be more complex than a graph.

23. Because there are only three points on the graph, the figure is a triangle.

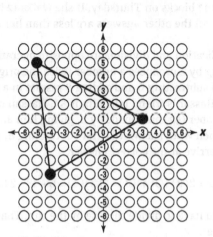

© John Wiley & Sons, Inc.

TIP

Questions where you mark your answer on the quadrant plane come up from time to time on the GED. Good mousing skills are essential to answering these questions correctly.

24. **24.** You can represent the ladder leaning against a house as a right triangle with an hypotenuse of 25 feet and a base of 7 feet. You can use the Pythagorean Theorem to solve this problem. The Pythagorean Theorem states that $a^2 + b^2 = c^2$, where c is the measure of the hypotenuse. You can set up the problem as $25^2 = 7^2 + \text{height}^2$ and solve for the height. You can simplify to $625 - 49 = \text{height}^2$. The answer is $24 = \text{height}$. (The square root of 576 is 24.)

REMEMBER

Pythagoras, a Greek mathematician, is credited with the discovery that the square of the hypotenuse of a right-angled triangle is equal to the sum of the squares of the other two sides. The *hypotenuse* is the side opposite the right angle. You'll find the Pythagorean Theorem on the formula sheet you get with your test.

The Pythagorean Theorem is frequently tested on the GED, so it pays to understand how to use it.

TIP

25. **D. 4 units to the left of the *y*-axis.** All points with *x*-coordinates that are negative are located to the left of the *y*-axis (the vertical axis). Therefore, if a point has an *x*-coordinate of −4, it's located on a line 4 units to the left of the *y*-axis.

26. **C. 1 year.** The average age for women claiming Social Security increased from 63.6 to 64.6 during that period. That's an increase of exactly 1 year, which makes Choice (C) the correct answer. This item shows that it pays to read the information and the question carefully and focus only on the information needed to answer the question. In this case, you only need to pay attention to the information about women. That's why Choice (D) is incorrect. Choice (D) shows the increase for men.

27. **A. makes it two times larger.** In this linear equation, any multiple of one term results in the same multiple of the answer. Multiplying *l* by 2 results in increasing *A* by 2.

28. **C. 160.** You can use the formula for area to calculate the number of square feet Herman has to cover in primer. The dimensions of the wall are 20 feet by 8 feet, which is 160 square feet. If your first choice for the answer was Choice (A), you added the length and height instead of multiplying. If you picked Choice (B), you confused perimeter with area. Remember that *perimeter* is the distance all the way around an object — in this case, $2(20+8)=56$. Choice (D) is the answer with the first two digits reversed. This item is a good illustration of making sure that you use the correct formula (in this case, area of a rectangle, not perimeter) and then apply it correctly. It's also a good reminder to select your answer carefully. Reversing digits under the stress of time limits isn't impossible or unusual.

29. **B. four units to the left and four units below the corresponding axis.** Because both coordinates are negative, the point would have to be the corresponding distance to the left and below the corresponding axis.

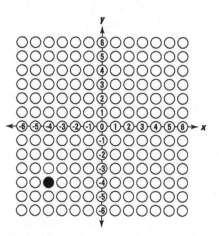

© John Wiley & Sons, Inc.

30. **30.00.** If you use x to represent the amount of money Roger spent, the amount of money that Ekua spent is $2x$. You can represent their total spending by the equation $90 = x + 2x$ or $3x = 90$, in which case $x = 30$. So Roger spent $30.00 for clothing.

Block 4

Taking a (Shortened) Practice Test

Taking a practice test is one of the most important parts of preparing for the GED. To help you prepare for the GED in 5 hours, this practice test is shorted from 7 hours down to 3 hours, 5 minutes. The only part that is the same time as the actual GED is the Extended Response because writing half an essay wouldn't be that helpful.

REMEMBER

On the real GED, you'll take the test on a computer. Instead of marking your answers on an answer sheet, like you do for the practice tests in this book, you'll use the keyboard and the mouse to indicate your answers. I formatted the questions and answer choices in this book to make them appear as similar as possible to what you'll see on the computer screen, but I had to retain some A, B, C, and D choices and provide an answer sheet for marking your answers. If possible, write the essay on a computer to simulate conditions on test day. Have one or two sheets of paper to use to jot down notes and organize your ideas.

Use the timer on your phone to keep track of time. If you run out of time, mark the last question you answered. Then answer the rest of the questions. This will help you figure out how much more quickly you will have to work to complete the entire test in the time allowed.

When you're done with the practice tests, you can find the answers and explanations at the end of this block. Just look for the relevant section in the "Answers and Explanations" section. After you check your answers, you can use any extra preparation time you have to review the concepts in the questions you missed so that you're ready for the GED.

Reasoning through Language Arts Practice Test

The following sections include practice questions for all parts of the GED Reasoning through Language Arts test. To make it simpler for you to time yourself, I present the questions for the Reading Comprehension and Grammar and Language components together in one section rather than separately (as on the real GED), with the Extended Response at the end of the test.

Reading comprehension and grammar and usage

1. _____   11. _____   21. _____

2. _____   12. _____   22. _____

3. _____   13. _____   23. _____

4. _____   14. _____   24. _____

5. _____   15. _____   25. _____

6. _____   16. _____   26. _____

7. _____   17. _____   27. _____

8. _____   18. _____   28. _____

9. _____   19. _____   29. _____

10. _____   20. _____   30. _____

TIME: 35 minutes

QUESTIONS: 30

DIRECTIONS: You may answer the questions in this section in any order. Mark your answers on the answer sheet provided.

Questions 1–8 refer to the following excerpt from Jack London's "In a Far Country" (1899).

(1) When the world rang with the tale of Arctic gold, and the lure of the North gripped the heartstrings of men, Carter Weatherbee threw up his snug clerkship, turned the half of his savings over to his wife, and with the remainder bought an outfit. There was no romance in his nature — the bondage of commerce had crushed all that; he was simply tired of the ceaseless grind, and wished to risk great hazards in view of corresponding returns . . . and there, unluckily for his soul's welfare, he allied himself with a party of men.

(2) There was nothing unusual about this party, except its plans. Even its goal, like that of all the other parties, was the Klondike. But the route it had mapped out to attain that goal took away the breath of the hardiest native, born and bred to the vicissitudes of the Northwest. Even Jacques Baptiste, born of a Chippewa woman and a renegade voyageur (having raised his first whimpers in a deerskin lodge north of the sixty-fifth parallel, and had the same hushed by blissful sucks of raw tallow), was surprised. Though he sold his services to them and agreed to travel even to the never-opening ice, he shook his head ominously whenever his advice was asked.

(3) Percy Cuthfert's evil star must have been in the ascendant, for he, too, joined this company of Argonauts. He was an ordinary man, with a bank account as deep as his culture, which is saying a good deal. He had no reason to embark on such a venture — no reason in the world, save that he suffered from an abnormal development of sentimentality. He mistook this for the true spirit of romance and adventure.

1. Which of the following words or phrases describes Carter Weatherbee?

   (A) romantic

   (B) a hardy native

   (C) willing to take a risk for a good return

   (D) a hero

2. What was meant by "bondage of commerce" in this sentence in Paragraph 1?

   There was no romance in his nature — the bondage of commerce had crushed all that; he was simply tired of the ceaseless grind, and wished to risk great hazards in view of corresponding returns . . . and there, unluckily for his soul's welfare, he allied himself with a party of men.

   (A) the corresponding returns

   (B) the romance of his nature

   (C) the drudgery of life as a clerk

   (D) the risk of great hazards

3. What was the goal of the party?

   (A) to find the old trails

   (B) to reach the Klondike

   (C) to map out a route

   (D) to tell the tale of the Arctic

4. Which word best describes the chosen route to the Klondike?

   (A) blissful

   (B) hardy

   (C) scenic

   (D) ominous

5. Why was Jacques Baptiste important to the party?

   (A) He was born of a Chippewa woman.

   (B) He was a renegade voyager.

   (C) He was born in a deerskin lodge.

   (D) He was a native of the Northwest.

6. According to the passage, what was unusual about the group?

   (A) their proposed route

   (B) their desire to find gold

   (C) their destination

   (D) their use of a local guide

7. Why do you think Percy Cuthfert joined the party?

   (A) to show that he is an ordinary man

   (B) because of his evil nature

   (C) to seek romance and adventure

   (D) to get rich

8. Based on the hints the author gives, how will the story likely end for Carter Weatherbee?

   (A) It will be a triumphant success.

   (B) He will escape with only his life.

   (C) He will die on the journey.

   (D) He will break even and make it home safely.

Questions 9–14 refer to this passage from a website.

Social Security _____ financial protection for our nation's people for over 80 years. Chances are, you either receive Social _____ someone who does. With retirement, disability, and _____ benefits, Social Security is one of the most successful anti-poverty programs in our nation's history.

We are passionate about supporting our customers by delivering financial support, providing superior _____ the safety and security of your information — helping you secure today and tomorrow.

Social Security is committed to helping maintain the basic well-being and protection of the people we serve. We pay benefits to about 64 million people including retirees, children, widows, and widowers. From birth, to marriage, and into _____ are there to provide support throughout life's journey.

One of our priorities is getting you secure access to the information you need when, where, and how you need it. Whether it is in person, on the phone, or through your personal *my* Social Security _____ are committed to providing superior customer service to put you in control.

9. Social Security _____ financial protection for our nation's people for more than 80 years.

   (A) has provided

   (B) provided

   (C) provides

   (D) providing

10. Chances are, you either receive Social _____ someone who does.

    (A) Security or know

    (B) Security, or know

    (C) security or know

    (D) Security or knew

11. With retirement, disability, and _____ benefits, Social Security is one of the most successful anti-poverty programs in our nation's history.

    (A) survivors

    (B) survivors'

    (C) survivor's

    (D) survivors's

12. We are passionate about supporting our customers by delivering financial support, providing superior _____ the safety and security of your information — helping you secure today and tomorrow.

    (A) customer service. And safeguarding

    (B) customer service, and safeguarding

    (C) customer, service and safeguarding

    (D) customer, service, and safeguarding

13. From birth, to marriage, and into _____ are there to provide support throughout life's journey.

    (A) retirement we

    (B) retirement, we

    (C) retiring, we

    (D) retiring we

14. Whether it is in person, on the phone, or through your personal *my* Social Security _____ are committed to providing superior customer service to put you in control.

    (A) account, we

    (B) account we

    (C) account. We

    (D) account,

Dear Customer,

We are writing to provide you with information on some important updates to your Cash Back Advantage credit card account. Effective March 1, we will stop offering _____. On this date your account _____ to our exciting, new Unlimited Cash Back credit card. Your new card will keep all the _____ card but will have several improvements and new features.

Effective March 1, you will receive unlimited 1% cash back on all purchases _____ you use the card. _____ you received 1% percent cash back at supermarkets and filling stations, and 0.5% everywhere else. Now you can get the same high cash back rate on all your purchases, including purchases made in drug stores, warehouse clubs, and online. _____ you shop!

Effective March 1, our new Warranty Plus plan will double the manufacturer's warranty on all major purchases. If your new computer has a year-long warranty, we will double it to two years. This plan applies to any purchase over $200 that comes with a warranty. Do you need a new washing machine? A new computer? A new TV? They're all covered! This coverage does not apply to used or second-hand items.

Effective March 1, you will also get free insurance for your mobile phone. We will repair or replace your mobile phone as long as you pay your monthly phone bill _____. Pay your phone bill with your card, and you're covered for that month. It's that easy!

All these benefits are waiting for you. _____ new card will arrive in the mail in the next few weeks.

15. Effective March 1, we will stop offering _____.

   (A) this card

   (B) that

   (C) it to nobody

   (D) them

16. On this date your account _____ to our exciting, new Unlimited Cash Back credit card.

   (A) would transition

   (B) had transitioned

   (C) will transition

   (D) transitioned

17. Your new card will keep all the _____ card but will have several improvements and new features.

   (A) grate features of your old

   (B) great features of your old

   (C) grate feature of your old

   (D) great feature of your old

18. Effective March 1, you will receive unlimited 1% cash back on all purchases
_____ you use the card.

(A) wherever and anywhere

(B) whenever and anywhere

(C) whoever

(D) every time

19. _____ you received 1% percent cash back at supermarkets and filling stations, and 0.5% everywhere else.

(A) Subsequently,

(B) Simultaneously,

(C) Previously,

(D) Unfortunately,

20. _____ you shop!

(A) Everywhere

(B) You get that rate everywhere

(C) That rate is gotten

(D) You are being given that rate everywhere

21. We will repair or replace your mobile phone as long as you pay your monthly phone bill
_____.

(A) on time using your card

(B) using your card on time

(C) on time and using your card

(D) and on time using your card

22. _____ new card will arrive in the mail in the next few weeks.

(A) your

(B) You're

(C) That

(D) Your

Questions 23–30 refer to this article.

Energy drinks are a very popular and growing segment of the beverage industry. In a recent year, sales of these invigorating drinks reached $57 billion worldwide. Next to multivitamins, energy drinks are the most _____ consumed nutritional supplement among American teenagers and young adults. _____ health experts warn that these drinks can pose a number of health risks.

First, energy drinks contain large amounts of sugar. Just 8 ounces of an energy drink, on average, _____ around 30 g of sugar. A single 16-ounce can of energy drink exceeds the recommended daily amount of added sugar in our diet for both men and women. Excessive sugar can cause a number of heart problems. It can also lead to weight gain and diabetes. Sugary drinks also promote tooth decay. Sugar-free and zero-calorie energy drinks avoid this sugar but contain artificial sweeteners with risks of their own.

Second, energy drinks usually contain large amounts of caffeine. Caffeine, a stimulant, makes us feel alert and awake. At low levels, caffeine is thought to have a number of health benefits. Most experts agree that caffeine can improve memory, increase alertness, and give us energy. Experts agree that for most people, _____. However, a large can of some energy drinks can contain up to 250 mg of caffeine. In contrast, a cup of coffee contains 100 mg of caffeine or less and a can of cola contains less than 50 mg of caffeine. Excessive amounts of caffeine _____ our nervous systems and hearts. In a single four-year period, emergency room visits associated with energy drinks doubled, with a significant number requiring hospitalization. Some emergency room doctors have noted an association of energy drink consumption with heart attacks. Caffeine can also disrupt our sleep patterns, causing more fatigue in the days after consuming the drinks. In addition, excessive caffeine can make us feel jumpy, nervous, or irritable — the "caffeine jitters" people sometimes talk about. Dehydration is another negative consequence of caffeine intake. _____ the body removes caffeine from the system, water goes with it. _____ from caffeine make these drinks particularly risky when exercising. The drinks are also associated with unsteadiness of the hands, which adds additional risk when weight training. Before, during, and after exercise, the best drink is plain, ordinary water.

Energy drinks may also contain other herbs and supplements, such as guarana, ginseng, taurine, glucuronolactone, and bitter orange. While people have taken most of these substances for centuries, their health benefits are unproven. In addition, some of these exotic ingredients may have unknown or unusual side effects for some people.

Clearly, energy drinks pose a number of health risks. Good, old ordinary water is a much better alternative. And if you need some _____ a healthful snack, such as an apple or banana, a handful of nuts, or some raisins.

23. Next to multivitamins, energy drinks are the most _____ consumed nutritional supplement among American teenagers and young adults.

   (A) frequent

   (B) frequently

   (C) usual

   (D) popular

24. _____ health experts warn that these drinks can pose a number of health risks.

   (A) Instead,

   (B) In addition,

   (C) And

   (D) But

25. Just 8 ounces of an energy drink, on average, _____ around 30 g of sugar.

   (A) contains

   (B) contain

   (C) contained

   (D) had contained

26. Experts agree that for most people, _____.

    (A) safely consuming up to 400 mg of caffeine per day

    (B) up to 400 mg of caffeine are safe to consume

    (C) it's safe to consume up to 400 mg of caffeine per day

    (D) its safe to consume up to 400 mg of caffeine per day

27. Excessive amounts of caffeine _____ our nervous systems and hearts.

    (A) can effect

    (B) can affect

    (C) effects

    (D) affects

28. _____ the body removes caffeine from the system, water goes with it.

    (A) Because

    (B) During

    (C) As

    (D) Before

29. _____ from caffeine make these drinks particularly risky when exercising.

    (A) Dehydration coupled with increased heart rate and blood pressure

    (B) Dehydration, increased heart rate, and blood pressure

    (C) Dehydration, heart rate, and increased blood pressure

    (D) Dehydration and heart rate and blood pressure

30. And if you need some _____ a healthful snack, such as an apple or banana, a handful of nuts, or some raisins.

    (A) energy, try

    (B) energy try

    (C) energy. Try

    (D) energy; try

At this point, you may take a 10-minute break before beginning the Extended Response.

Extended Response

TIME: 45 minutes

YOUR ASSIGNMENT: The following articles present arguments from both supporters and critics of video games. In your response, analyze both positions presented in the two articles to determine which one is best supported. Use relevant and specific evidence from the articles to support your response. If possible, write your essay on a computer with spell-check, grammar-check, and autocorrect turned off. Otherwise, use the following sheets of lined paper to prepare your response. Spend up to 45 minutes reading the passages and planning, writing, revising, and editing your response.

Article 1 **Video Games Are Harmful**

While playing video games can be seen as a fun pastime, these games actually are at the root of a number of social problems.

Studies show that violent video games encourage violence and violent behavior. In fact, the high level of violence in these games has even garnered the attention of a U.S. Supreme Court Justice, who was astounded by the deaths, injuries, and weapons depicted in popular games. Many experts note a correlation between increased video game playing and violence in the United States.

Video games also encourage a sedentary lifestyle. With obesity at an all-time high, people should be exercising, playing sports, or working out. They should not be seated at their computer or lying on their couch, playing games for hours on end.

Experts warn that video games can become addictive and also cause injury. It's not uncommon for players to sit for hours, day after day, playing games. Experts believe that playing games to relax or unwind can pull your focus away from important priorities, such as work, school, home, and family. In addition, playing video games for hours on end has resulted in a large increase in repetitive stress injuries, which can be painful and debilitating. One common injury is called "video game thumb," which occurs because players use their thumbs so much to play.

For all these reasons, people are better off cutting back or eliminating video games, and engaging in other, more positive pastimes, such as exercising, listening to music, enjoying hobbies, or spending time with their families and friends.

Article 2 **Video Games Score High**

While many people are against video games, video games actually provide a lot of benefits to those who play them.

Video games teach important values such as teamwork, competition, and fair play. When you play a video game, you don't just play alone. You play with a friend or friends in the same room, or connected online. This way, players learn valuable skills needed for teamwork, including cooperation and communication. These skills are highly valued in the workplace today. Players also learn the value of competition as they compete against each other to win. And finally, players learn about fair play. Playing a video game involves following the rules. Playing fair, being a gracious winner, and not being a sore loser are all valuable skills players can use in other areas of their lives.

Video games also develop players' imaginations. Video games take place in a variety of interesting and exotic situations. While playing, players become immersed in an imaginative world full of color, action, and adventure. Some video games are so imaginative that they have been made into movies or rides at amusement parks. While people complain about the violence in video games, no reputable scientific study has shown a connection between watching video games and engaging in real-world violence.

Video games also provide a lot of fun, safe entertainment. Playing video games provides hours of fun without having to leave your home. These days, that is an important consideration.

Video games also have a massive economic impact. They generate billions of dollars of revenue and create thousands of jobs. Because these games are popular overseas, they are an important export, too.

Moreover, there is an important question of rights. Who has the right to stop video games or control their content? That's censorship! Video games come with maturity ratings, and families need to monitor their children's use of them. But banning them or banning certain content is not the American way!

Finally, video games are just plain fun. For many people, video games provide moments of entertainment and relaxation. They can forget their problems and enjoy a few minutes of distraction from their everyday problems. What's wrong with that?

For all these reasons, video games are a fun, useful, and important part of our culture. I think that all the people who don't like video games should try one. It might change their minds.

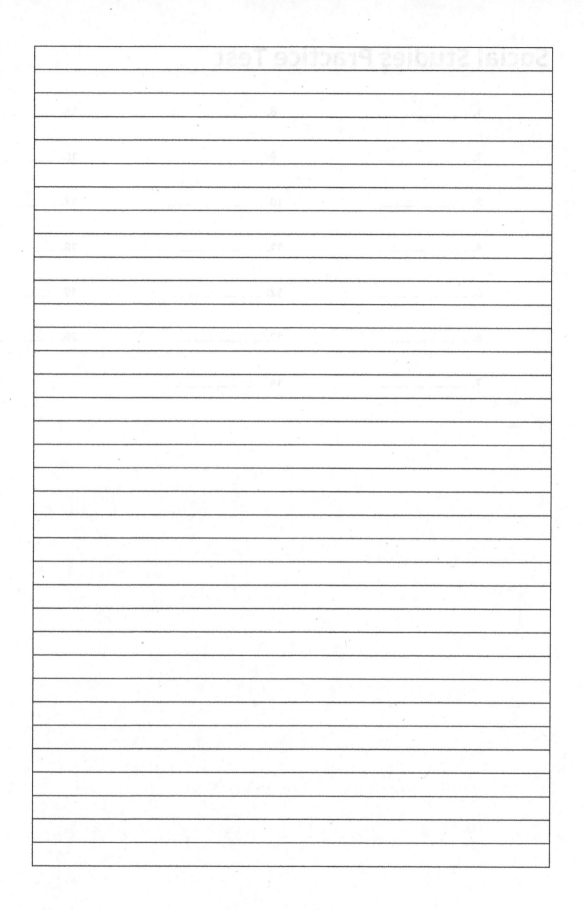

Social Studies Practice Test

1. _____

2. _____

3. _____

4. _____

5. _____

6. _____

7. _____

8. _____

9. _____

10. _____

11. _____

12. _____

13. _____

14. _____

15. _____

16. _____

17. _____

18. _____

19. _____

20. _____

Questions 1–3 refer to an excerpt from a speech on voting rights for women that Mark Twain gave to an audience of women employed in New York factories and an excerpt from the U.S. Constitution.

Votes for Women (1901)
By Mark Twain

Referring to woman's sphere in life, I'll say that woman is always right. For twenty-five years I've been a woman's rights man. I have always believed, long before my mother died, that, with her gray hairs and admirable intellect, perhaps she knew as much as I did. Perhaps she knew as much about voting as I.

I should like to see the time come when women shall help to make the laws. I should like to see that whiplash, the ballot, in the hands of women. As for this city's government, I don't want to say much, except that it is a shame — a shame; but if I should live twenty-five years longer — and there is no reason why I shouldn't — I think I'll see women handle the ballot. If women had the ballot today, the state of things in this town would not exist.

If all the women in this town had a vote today they would elect a mayor at the next election, and they would rise in their might and change the awful state of things now existing here.

19th Amendment (1920)

The right of citizens of the United States to vote shall not be denied or abridged by the United States or by any State on account of sex. Congress shall have power to enforce this article by appropriate legislation.

1. What was the purpose of Twain's speech?

   (A) He wanted to end corruption in New York.

   (B) He wanted to show support for women's suffrage.

   (C) He wanted to encourage equal access to education.

   (D) He wanted to praise his mother.

2. Which of the following is an opinion?

   (A) Twain supported voting rights for women.

   (B) The 19th Amendment was ratified in 1920.

   (C) Women are better at stopping corruption than men.

   (D) In 1901, people were concerned about corruption in New York government.

3. Which of the following does the 19th Amendment demonstrate?

   (A) When women started to vote, corruption in politics decreased.

   (B) When women were able to vote, they could only vote in federal elections.

   (C) Women received the right to vote sooner than Twain predicted.

   (D) The federal government was unwilling to enforce women's right to vote.

4. In 1973, after 19 years of direct involvement, the United States ended its involvement in the Vietnam War. President Richard Nixon called the treaty that ended the war "peace with honor." By 1975, Vietnam, Cambodia, and Laos all fell under Communist rule. Which of these statements is a conclusion that can be drawn from this information?

(A) Capitalism is a better system than Communism.

(B) The Communist forces in Vietnam honored the treaty.

(C) The U.S.-backed government in South Vietnam was stronger than the Communist regime in the North.

(D) U.S. involvement in the war was a failure.

5. The Federalist Papers were a series of newspaper articles published anonymously in support of ratifying the U.S. Constitution. The authors were prominent patriots. Federalist Number 10, by James Madison, said, "The instability, injustice, and confusion introduced into the public councils, have, in truth, been the mortal diseases under which popular governments have everywhere perished; as they continue to be the favorite and fruitful topics from which the adversaries to liberty derive their most specious declamations."

Which of the following would Madison most likely believe is a threat to democracy?

(A) a TV news report about controversy in Congress over a new spending bill

(B) a newspaper article about the release of an official U.S. government study of UFOs

(C) a series of social media posts saying that the army is secretly getting ready to take over Washington, D.C.

(D) an Internet news story on ways that diverse Americans exercise their religious freedom

Question 6 refers to the following passage and table.

Executive orders are instructions the president can issue. The Constitution grants the president the right to issue executive orders on how to enforce laws or how to use federal resources. Other times, specific laws give the president latitude on how to implement the law. This table shows the number of executive orders issued by recent U.S. presidents.

Executive Orders Issued by Recent U.S. Presidents

President	Terms	Number of Executive Orders	Average Per Year
William J. Clinton	2	305	38
George W. Bush	2	291	36
Barack H. Obama	2	276	35
Donald J. Trump	1	219	55

Source: Adapted from Federal Register

6. Which of the following statements can be concluded from this information?

(A) One-term presidents tend to issue more executive orders than two-term presidents.

(B) President Trump issued more executive orders per year than the other three presidents in the table.

(C) Presidents tend to issue more executive orders in their first terms than their second terms.

(D) Executive orders have declined over the years.

7. Civil rights and political rights are two ways to classify people's rights. Civil rights guarantee people's lives and safety as well as freedoms of religion, speech, and other important rights. Political rights include people's legal rights (such as right to a fair trial) and rights to participate in government (such as the right to vote or to protest the actions of the government). Which of the following people is using their civil rights?

(A) Mandy distributes flyers in support of a certain school board candidate.

(B) Seema attends weekly prayers at her local mosque.

(C) David writes a letter to his representative in Congress to complain about a new proposed law.

(D) Frank is visiting his daughter in another state, so he votes using an absentee ballot.

8. State voting patterns are often discussed in terms of red states or blue states, depending on which party they usually vote for.

Which statement can be concluded from the map?

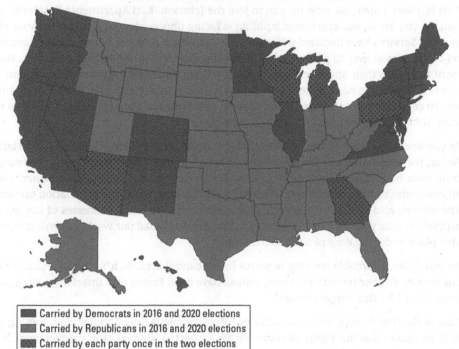

Red States and Blue States in Recent Elections

Carried by Democrats in 2016 and 2020 elections
Carried by Republicans in 2016 and 2020 elections
Carried by each party once in the two elections

(A) American voters are very concerned about the future of the country.

(B) Democrats are strong in rural and agricultural areas.

(C) Purple states are disloyal to their parties.

(D) Voting patterns show that the United States is very divided politically.

9. Under the U.S. Constitution, the legislative branch (1) _____ laws and the (2) _____ branch interprets the laws.

- enforces
- enacts
- interprets
- removes
- legislative
- judicial
- executive
- military

Questions 10–11 refer to the following letter.

Dear Residents of the Johnson-Earl Apartments:

This is a very important time for you to join the Johnson-Earl Apartments Residents' Association. As you know, our apartment building is facing unprecedented changes because of the new owners. Services have declined while rent has increased. Some of our members have received rent increases of over 10 percent when renewing their leases. When they move out, the management renovates their apartments and converts them into luxury apartments that rent for much more. Management has frequently retained tenants' damage deposits, even though their plan was to completely gut the apartment. Clearly, management's goal is to force all of us out of our long-time homes and keep our damage deposits.

As you know, the Association believes that management's actions violate city and state laws. So far, the association has filed five suits on behalf of individual tenants who are being forced from their homes, in addition to a class-action lawsuit against the building owners on behalf of all residents. You can find all the latest news and updates about the association on our website. The website also contains the names, phone numbers, and email addresses of key government officials in case you want to contact them. You can download our weekly newsletter, which we also place under the door of each apartment.

As you know, affordable housing is scarce in the capital area, so it's essential that we fight for our homes. Former tenants who have moved have been forced into inferior housing in unsafe areas. Don't let this happen to you!

Now is the time to support the association. Membership is only $20 per year. Joining now will help us ensure that our rights as residents are respected. Help us stop management from taking your home. Join today!

Sincerely,

Marta Obredor,

President, Johnson-Earl Residents' Association

10. Why does the president of the association add information about problems tenants face after they move out?

   (A) so tenants will ask the government to build more affordable housing

   (B) to add urgency to her message

   (C) to make management aware of the association's concerns

   (D) to convince management to abandon its plan for the building

11. Which right or freedom in the U.S. Constitution supports the association and its activities?

   (A) freedom of religion

   (B) the right to bear arms

   (C) the right to petition for redress of grievances

   (D) the right to a fair and speedy trial

Questions 12–13 refer to the following information.

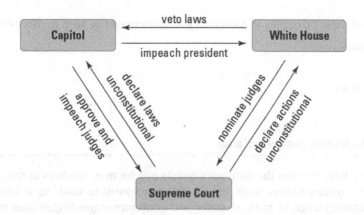

12. What is the purpose of this system?

   (A) to ensure that the president does not become too powerful

   (B) to ensure that the budget is balanced

   (C) to prevent one part of government from becoming too powerful

   (D) to ensure the rule of law

13. What do this system and the Bill of Rights have in common?

   (A) They are both in the Declaration of Independence.

   (B) They both support freedom of religion.

   (C) They both give the government too much power.

   (D) They are both limitations on the power of the federal government.

Question 14 refers to this drawing, attributed to Benjamin Franklin, which is believed to be the first political cartoon. First used in the French and Indian Wars, it later was used during the Revolutionary War.

Source: The Library of Congress / Wikimedia Commons / Public domain

14. The origin of which of these principles of American government can be seen in this cartoon?

(A) separation of powers

(B) federalism

(C) freedom to bear arms

(D) rule of law

Question 15 refers to the following passage and table.

The federal minimum wage law sets the minimum hourly pay for most workers in the United States. Tipped workers receive a lower wage, but the difference must be made up in tips. States may set a higher minimum wage. In 2021, 29 states had minimum wages higher than the federal minimum wage. Here is information about the history of the federal minimum wage.

Recent Increases to the U.S. Minimum Wage

Year of Increase	Minimum Wage
1981	$3.35
1990	$3.80
1991	$4.25
1996	$4.75
1997	$5.15
2007	$5.85
2008	$6.65
2009	$7.25

15. Which year saw the largest increase in the minimum wage?

(A) 1997

(B) 2007

(C) 2008

(D) 2009

Question 16 refers to the following passage.

The Great Recession was a widespread global economic slowdown that occurred between 2007 and 2009. Economists consider this event to be the second-biggest downturn in history since the Great Depression of the 1930s. The Great Recession was triggered in large part by a collapse of housing prices in the United States. Many mortgages were backed by subprime mortgages issued to less-than-qualified buyers on homes that frequently had an inflated value. When the homeowners were unable to pay, housing prices declined and the value of the bonds backing those mortgages collapsed. The result was a dramatic economic downturn felt especially in North America, Europe, and South America.

16. What is one of the reasons mortgage-backed securities were a problem?

(A) They provided financing for mortgages.

(B) They were based on mortgages issued to people with poor credit.

(C) Their collateral was real estate.

(D) They were a new kind of investment security.

17. A monopoly is a company that controls a large segment of a particular product or market to the detriment of other companies, consumers, and the economy as a whole. Certain companies, such as utilities, are exempt from laws designed to prevent monopolies.

Which of the following would be considered an illegal monopoly?

(A) a water company that provides water to every home and business in a certain city

(B) an online ad provider that controls most Internet advertising

(C) the top-rated TV network in the United States

(D) a publicly operated toll road that is the only practical route linking three states

Questions 18–19 refer to the following excerpt from a speech that former Prime Minister Winston Churchill delivered in Fulton, Missouri, in 1946, shortly after the end of World War II.

A shadow has fallen upon the scenes so lately lighted by the Allied victory. Nobody knows what Soviet Russia and its Communist international organization intends to do in the immediate future or what are the limits if any to their expansive and proselytizing tendencies. I have a strong admiration and regards for the valiant Russian people and for my wartime comrade, Marshal Stalin. There is sympathy and goodwill in Britain — and I doubt not here also — towards the peoples of all the Russia and a resolve to preserve through many differences and rebuffs in establishing lasting friendships. We understand the Russian need to be secure on her western frontiers by the removal of all possibility of German aggression. We welcome Russia to her rightful place among the leading nations of the world. Above all we welcome constant, frequent and growing contacts between the Russian people and our own people on both sides of the Atlantic. It is my duty however, for I am sure you would wish me to state the facts as I see them to you, to place before you certain facts about the present position in Europe.

From Stettin in the Baltic to Trieste in the Adriatic, an "iron curtain" has descended across the continent. Behind that line lie all the capitals of the ancient states of Central and Eastern Europe. Warsaw, Berlin, Prague, Vienna, Budapest, Belgrade, Bucharest and Sofia; all these famous cities and the populations around them lie in what I must call the Soviet sphere, and all are subject in one form or another, not only to Soviet influence but to a very high and, in many cases, increasing measure of control from Moscow. Athens alone — Greece with its immortal glories — is free to decide its future at an election under British, American, and French observation. The Russian-dominated Polish Government has been encouraged to make enormous and wrongful inroads upon Germany, and mass expulsions of millions of Germans on a scale grievous and undreamed-of are now taking place. The Communist parties, which were very small in all these Eastern States of Europe, have been raised to pre-eminence and power far beyond their numbers and are seeking everywhere to obtain totalitarian control. Police governments are prevailing in nearly every case, and so far, except in Czechoslovakia, there is no true democracy.

18. Which choice best describes the relationship between Churchill and Stalin at the time of this speech?

   (A) Churchill respects Stalin as an ally but fears his present intentions.

   (B) Churchill believes Stalin knows the best way forward for Europe.

   (C) Churchill has always distrusted Stalin.

   (D) Churchill believes that the Allies should never have accepted the Soviet Union as a partner in the war.

19. What does Churchill mean when he talks about an "Iron Curtain"?

   (A) Russia built a wall of steel between countries it controlled and the rest of Europe.

   (B) Europe has been divided into one area with democratic governments and another under Communist dictatorships.

   (C) The Soviet Union has incorporated several former countries in Europe into its borders.

   (D) Countries under Communist rule are as free as countries in the rest of Europe.

Question 20 refers to the following passage.

The number of refugees in the world is at an all-time high. This decade began with nearly double the number of refugees than just ten years before. Most refugees are fleeing war or violence, but others are seeking food security or water security. The main countries that refugees are fleeing from include Burundi, Eritrea, Central African Republic, Sudan, Democratic Republic of Congo, Somalia, Burma, South Sudan, Afghanistan, and Syria. While governments, international organizations, and NGOs (non-government organizations) work to assist refugees, these migrants often find themselves living in difficult circumstances in their new locations. Many are in large camps living in poor conditions. In addition to these refugees, there are also record numbers of internally displaced people, such as people in Eastern Ukraine fleeing Russia-supported invaders.

20. Of the countries mentioned in the information, which continent are most of them located in?

   (A) Middle East

   (B) Asia

   (C) Europe

   (D) Africa

Science Practice Test

1. _____   7. _____   13. _____

2. _____   8. _____   14. _____

3. _____   9. _____   15. _____

4. _____   10. _____   16. _____

5. _____   11. _____   17. _____

6. _____   12. _____   18. _____

TIME: 30 minutes

QUESTIONS: 18

DIRECTIONS: Read each question carefully and mark your answer on the answer sheet provided.

Questions 1–2 refer to the following information.

Two parents have the following genotypes for eye color.

The parent with the Bb genotype has brown eyes. The parent with the bb genotype has blue eyes.

	b	b
B	B b	B b
b	b b	b b

A Punnett square for eye color

1. Which allele is dominant for eye color?

   (A) green

   (B) brown

   (C) blue

   (D) hazel

2. What are the odds that the parents will have a child with brown eyes?

   (A) 1:4

   (B) 2:4

   (C) 3:4

   (D) 4:4

3. The piping plover is a small shorebird that nests on beaches. This species is found primarily in wetlands in the Dakotas, the Great Lakes, and the Atlantic shore. In winter they migrate to the Gulf Coast but have also been seen further south. Scientists estimate that their population is 7,800 to 8,400 individuals. They are considered endangered in the Great Lakes region and threatened in the Atlantic shore region.

   Which of the following would help conserve the piping plover population?

   (A) Decrease the number of wetlands in the Dakotas.

   (B) Protect other animals living in the nesting habitats.

   (C) Hold a plover information day at the nesting sites.

   (D) Prevent people from going into piping plovers' nesting habitats.

Question 4 refers to the following information.

Protozoa are single-cell organisms that are capable of movement. Two ways that they move are by using cilia and flagella. *Cilia* are short protrusions on the outside of the cell. The cilia beat together to move. A *flagella* is a single, tail-like protrusion that beats to move.

4. Write *cilia* or *flagella* to describe the illustration:

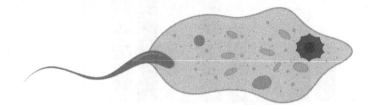

5. The lack of vitamin C can cause a disease called scurvy. Symptoms include tiredness, bone pain, skin problems, gum disease, and emotional changes. Scurvy was common on ships where sailors had little access to fresh food. Finally, in 1795, the British Navy realized that drinking lemon juice prevented scurvy. However, it was not until the 1930s that scientists discovered that a chemical, ascorbic acid, was the nutrient that prevented scurvy.

   Which of the following can be concluded from this information?

   (A) Correlation does not show cause.

   (B) Vitamin C is harmful because it's an acid.

   (C) Vitamin C is helpful so people should take doses many times the official RDA (recommended daily allowance).

   (D) The cause of scurvy is still unknown.

6. Systems of the human body have specialized functions. These systems work together to accomplish specific tasks. For example, the skeletal system and the muscular system work together to move the body.

   Which of these systems works with the respiratory system?

   (A) the skeletal system
   (B) the digestive system
   (C) the circulatory system
   (D) the immune system

Questions 7–8 refer to the following passage and illustration.

Students in a life science class are studying the effects of fertilizer. They plant two bean plants in flowerpots. They add a well-known garden fertilizer to one of the flowerpots. They give the plants the same amount of water and sunlight each day. They measure the plants each week and graph the results.

Effect of Fertilizer on Bean Plant Growth

7. What are the dependent and independent variables in this experiment?

    (A) independent — fertilizer, water, sunlight; dependent — plant height

    (B) independent — plant height; dependent — fertilizer

    (C) independent — fertilizer; dependent — water and sunlight

    (D) independent — fertilizer; dependent — plant height

8. Imagine that after measuring the plants in Week 4, one of the students notices that the plant without fertilizer doesn't receive full sunlight in the afternoon after school lets out. In the late afternoon, a shadow from a tree outside falls on only that plant. The class is going to repeat the experiment. What should the students do differently?

    (A) Rotate the flowerpots 180 degrees every day.

    (B) Increase the amount of water given to the plant without fertilizer.

    (C) Place both plants in places where light will not be blocked and switch the plants' positions once daily.

    (D) Place the plants in a window that is covered by a translucent shade to avoid drying out the plants from excessive sunlight.

9. Milk sickness was the cause of numerous deaths among settlers in the American Midwest. People became sick and died after drinking milk, but no one knew the cause. Anna Pierce Hobbs Bigsby, a respected local medical expert, believed a poisonous plant was responsible because the sickness never happened in winter months. Finally, an elderly Shawnee woman told her that the cause was a certain plant, white snakeroot. When cows ate that plant, the poison would enter their milk. Bigsby tested this hypothesis with a calf and found a correlation between cows consuming the plant and animals dying from drinking their milk. She tried to share her findings with people but her warnings were not taken seriously.

    Which of these is the most likely reason people did not take Bigsby's warning seriously?

    (A) At the time, people did not believe that certain plants were poisonous.

    (B) Bigsby did not use good research methods.

    (C) At the time, most of the medical community was not willing to pay attention to a woman.

    (D) People disliked Bigsby.

The amount of a substance that can dissolve in a liquid changes according to the temperature of the liquid. The graph shows the solubility curves for four substances.

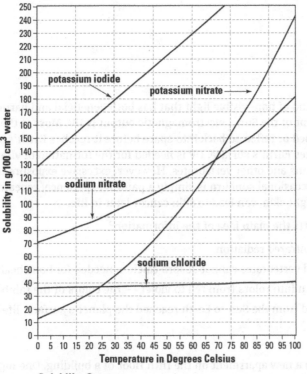

Solubility Curves

10. Which of the following can be inferred from the information in the graph?

    (A) The solubility of all four substances goes up as temperature increases.

    (B) The solubility of the four substances increases at the same rate.

    (C) Temperature does not affect solubility.

    (D) After 100°C, solubility will continue to increase.

11. Which substance's solubility increases the least as the temperature rises?

    (A) potassium iodide

    (B) sodium nitrate

    (C) potassium nitrate

    (D) sodium chloride

12. Newton's first law says that an object at rest will stay at rest and an object in motion will stay in motion unless acted upon by another force.

Which of the following is an example of an object being acted on by another force?

    (A) A baseball batter swings at a pitch and misses.

    (B) A child rolls a bowling ball and it comes to a stop part — way down the alley.

    (C) An antiques dealer stores a valuable antique vase in a locked display cabinet.

    (D) A meteor in space continues traveling in the same direction for millions of miles.

13. A simple machine changes the direction and/or strength of a force. Simple machines include a lever, a wheel and axle, a pulley, an inclined plane, a wedge, and a screw.

A hotel guest rolls a wheeled suitcase up a ramp into the hotel. Which simple machine are they using in addition to a wheel and axle?

(A) inclined plane

(B) wedge

(C) pulley

(D) lever

14. Ultraviolet (UV) light is a kind of non-visible light that has both beneficial and harmful effects for humans. About 10 percent of the Sun's electromagnetic output is UV. Most of the Sun's output, including UV, is absorbed or reflected back into space before it reaches Earth's surface. Only a small amount of UV reaches Earth's surface. UV is needed for the formation of vitamin D, a necessary nutrient, in humans and other vertebrates. However, excessive exposure to UV can lead to sunburn. While an occasional sunburn is simply a painful experience, repeated sunburns, especially for people with light skin, can lead to skin cancer later in life.

Which of these ideas supports the main idea of the information?

(A) Sunlight also contains infrared radiation.

(B) Without vitamin D, land vertebrates cannot absorb calcium needed for bone health.

(C) Visible light breaks down into colors from red to violet — the colors of the rainbow.

(D) If all the energy directed from the Sun to Earth reached the planet's surface, life on Earth would be impossible.

15. Peter has recently moved to a new apartment on the fifth floor of a building. One night, he realizes that he can hear the music from the nightclub on the first floor perfectly in his bedroom. His bedroom is in the back of the apartment, and the nightclub is in the front of the building. He does not hear the music in any other part of his apartment, in the elevator, or on the stairs.

Which of these statements explains why Peter can hear the music in his apartment?

(A) Sound waves are traveling through the air into his apartment through the window.

(B) Sound waves can travel through water.

(C) Sound waves are traveling through the stairway to his apartment.

(D) Sound waves can travel through solid materials.

16. Oceans absorb carbon dioxide in the air. As the amount of carbon dioxide in the atmosphere has increased, the amount of this gas dissolved in ocean waters has increased, too. In the ocean, carbon dioxide reacts to form carbonic acid.

What is a logical effect of this situation?

(A) The acidity of seawater will decline.

(B) The acidity of seawater will increase.

(C) The amount of carbon dioxide in the atmosphere will increase.

(D) The acidity of seawater will remain constant.

Question 17 refers to the following passage.

The five Great Lakes — Lake Superior, Lake Huron, Lake Michigan, Lake Ontario, and Lake Erie — comprise one of the world's largest freshwater systems. According to U.S. government statistics, they contain 84 percent of North America's surface fresh water, and 12 percent of the world's fresh water. Millions of people depend on water from these lakes. In addition to consuming the water, people use this water for power generation and transportation. The levels of the lakes are carefully monitored by government bodies in the United States and Canada. Lake levels were unusually high in several recent years. In August 2020, Lake Michigan was 33 inches above its average long-term level. While that may not seem like much, water levels that high can cause damage to buildings, docks, harbors, beaches, and roads. By 2021, water levels had dropped, but were still 22 inches above average. The level dropped more in 2022 but was expected to rise again. While an abundant supply of fresh water is good, too much water is harmful, too. Scientists attribute the increase to climate change and warn that cities such as Milwaukee and Chicago will suffer long-term consequences if lake levels continue to rise.

17. Which of the following can be concluded from the passage?

(A) Governments need to take steps to manage high water levels in Lake Michigan.

(B) Water levels will continue to drop from their high in 2020.

(C) High water levels are a bigger concern than low water levels.

(D) People who live along Lake Michigan do not need to worry about water security.

18. A scientist is studying the behavior of a large colony of bats that lives in an enormous cavern in Borneo. Scientific research has already determined that bats will not fly if the weather is rainy. The scientist wants to figure out if more bats will fly on dry nights after rainy weather than on dry nights following other dry nights. They plan on filming the bats each evening as they exit the cave to estimate the number of bats flying each night. They also believe that air temperature may affect how many bats fly, so they log the air temperature each day at the time the bats usually exit the cavern.

How many independent variables does this experiment have? Write the number. ☐

Math Practice Test

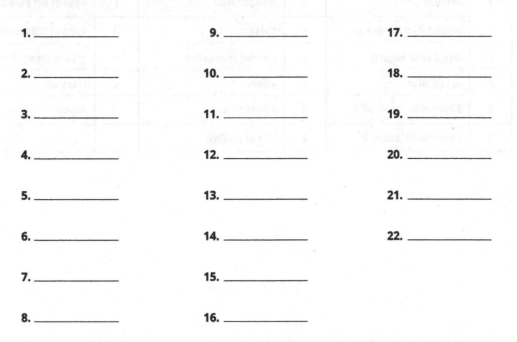

1. _____

2. _____

3. _____

4. _____

5. _____

6. _____

7. _____

8. _____

9. _____

10. _____

11. _____

12. _____

13. _____

14. _____

15. _____

16. _____

17. _____

18. _____

19. _____

20. _____

21. _____

22. _____

Mathematics Formula Explanations

This displays formulas relating to geometric measurement and certain algebra concepts and is available on the GED® test — Mathematical Reasoning.

Area of a:

square	$A = s^2$
rectangle	$A = lw$
parallelogram	$A = bh$
triangle	$A = \frac{1}{2}bh$
trapezoid	$A = \frac{1}{2}h(b_1 + b_2)$
circle	$A = \pi r^2$

Perimeter of a:

square	$P = 4s$
rectangle	$P = 2l + 2w$
triangle	$P = s_1 + s_2 + s_3$
Circumference of a circle	$C = 2\pi r$ OR $C = \pi d; \pi \approx 3.14$

Surface area and volume of a:

rectangular prism	$SA = 2lw + 2lh + 2wh$	$V = lwh$
right prism	$SA = ph + 2B$	$V = Bh$
cylinder	$SA = 2\pi rh + 2\pi r^2$	$V = \pi r^2 h$
pyramid	$SA = \frac{1}{2}ps + B$	$V = \frac{1}{3}Bh$
cone	$SA = \pi rs + \pi r^2$	$V = \frac{1}{3}\pi r^2 h$
sphere	$SA = 4\pi r^2$	$V = \frac{4}{3}\pi r^3$

(p = perimeter of base with area B; $\pi \approx 3.14$)

Data

mean	mean is equal to the total of the values of a data set, divided by the number of elements in the data set
median	median is the middle value in an odd number of ordered values of a data set, or the mean of the two middle values in an even number of ordered values in a data set

Algebra

slope of a line	$m = \dfrac{y_2 - y_1}{x_2 - x_1}$
slope-intercept form of the equation of a line	$y = mx + b$
point-slope form of the equation of a line	$y - y_1 = m(x - x_1)$
standard form of a quadratic equation	$y = ax^2 + bx + c$
quadratic formula	$x = \dfrac{-b \pm \sqrt{b^2 - 4ac}}{2a}$
Pythagorean theorem	$a^2 + b^2 = c^2$
simple interest	$I = Prt$
	(I = interest, P = principal, r = rate, t = time)
distance formula	$d = rt$
total cost	total cost = (number of units) x (price per unit)

Æ Symbol Tool Explanation

The GED® test on computer contains a tool known as the "Æ Symbol Tool." Use this guide to learn about entering special mathematical symbols into fill-in-the-blank item types.

Symbol	Explanation	Symbol	Explanation	Symbol	Explanation
π	pi	|	absolute value	—	minus or negative
f	function	×	multiplication	(	open or left parenthesis
$\geq$	greater than or equal to	÷	division	)	close or right parenthesis
$\leq$	less than or equal to	±	positive or negative	>	greater than
$\neq$	not equal to	∞	infinity	<	less than
2	2 exponent ("squared")	$\sqrt{}$	square root	=	equals
3	3 exponent ("cubed")	+	plus or positive		

TIME: 50 minutes

QUESTIONS: 22

DIRECTIONS: Find the answer to each question. Mark your answers on the answer sheet provided.

1. Jacob Smith searched for his name online to see how many results would come up. The search produced 354,000,000 results (and in under half a second, too!). If Jacob wrote this total as 3.54×10^x, the value of x would be _____.

2. You are one of 300 people who enter a lottery to get tickets to see your favorite recording artist. Tickets are numbered from 1 to 300. The lottery officials select every 15th person to get a ticket, starting with ticket number 8. Which of the following lottery numbers will also get a ticket?

   (A) 18
   (B) 88
   (C) 98
   (D) 108

3. $a = b^2 - (3 + 2c)$. Find a if $b = -3$, $c = -2$

   (A) −10
   (B) −9
   (C) 8
   (D) 10

4. Mercedes and Chen gather strawberries to make jam for the upcoming fall and winter. They gather A LOT of strawberries, enough to make 255 ounces of jam. They have an assortment of 3-, 6-, 12- and 24-ounce jars to put the jam in. Which combination of jars would contain all the jam that they made?

   (A) 15 3-oz. jars and 18 12-oz. jars
   (B) 7 6-oz. jars and 9 24-oz. jars
   (C) 13 3-oz. jars and 36 6-oz. jars
   (D) 13 18-oz. jars and 4 24-oz. jars

5. The local donut shop charges $0.89 for a single donut, $4.99 for a half-dozen donuts, and $9.49 for a dozen donuts. If you need to buy 36 donuts, how much would you save if you bought 3 dozen donuts as opposed to 36 individual donuts, before sales tax?

6. Jennie sees a new blouse at the store with a price tag of $20. When she goes to pay for it, she sees that the final cost after the tax is added is $21.20. What is the tax rate?

   (A) 1.2%
   (B) 5%
   (C) 6%
   (D) 12%

7. Caleb's normal commute to work takes about half an hour when he's driving in his car at an average rate of 40 mph. If he decided to take part in Bike-to-Work Day, how long would it take him to get to work if he averages 16 mph riding his bike?

(A) 1 hour, 15 minutes

(B) 1 hour, 25 minutes

(C) 1 hour, 40 minutes

(D) 2 hours, 30 minutes

8. The following line intercepts the y-axis at 4 and the x-axis at 5. What is the slope of the line?

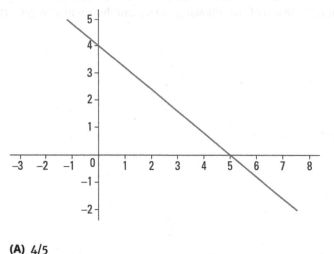

(A) 4/5

(B) −5/4

(C) −4/5

(D) 5/4

9. John's local pizza shop offers the following sizes of pizzas:

- 12-inch round pizza: $12.99

- 14-inch round pizza: $15.99

- 10 × 16-inch rectangular pizza: $17.99

Toppings cost $1 each. Drinks are sold for $2, $2.50, and $3 for S, M, and L, respectively.

If John has $20 to spend, which of the following orders can he NOT place? (Assume there is no tax or tip on the order.)

(A) a rectangular cheese pizza with a small drink

(B) a 14-inch pepperoni pizza with a medium drink

(C) a 12-inch green pepper, onion, and mushroom pizza with a large drink

(D) a 14-inch pineapple and ham pizza with a medium drink

10. Anthony gets paid $12 per hour to work at the local snack bar. If he works over 40 hours in a particular week, he gets paid 50% more per hour for those additional hours.

Suppose Anthony works 50 hours in one week. How much will he get paid for that week?

(A) $180

(B) $480

(C) $600

(D) $660

11. What is the least common multiple of 24 and 32?

(A) 8

(B) 96

(C) 128

(D) 192

Questions 12–13 refer to the following image.

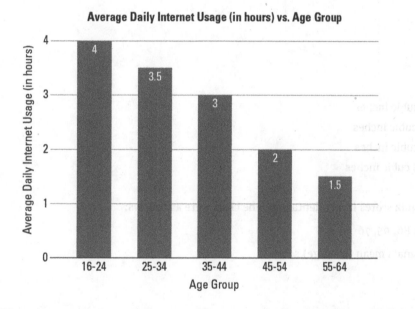

Average Daily Internet Usage (in hours) vs. Age Group

12. How many hours would you expect a 30-year-old to be online in the course of a 3-day weekend?

(A) 7

(B) 9

(C) 10.5

(D) 12

13. Between which two age groups was there the greatest difference in average daily Internet usage?

    (A) 16–24 and 25–34

    (B) 25–34 and 35–44

    (C) 35–44 and 45–54

    (D) 45–54 and 55–64

14. The cylinder in the figure shown here is inscribed in the square prism. They both have a height of 12 inches. The cylinder has a radius of 5 inches. What is the difference in volume between the prism and the cylinder?

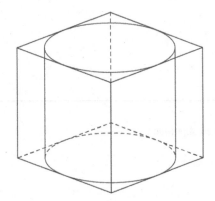

    (A) 257.5 cubic inches

    (B) 942.5 cubic inches

    (C) 1,200 cubic inches

    (D) 2,142.5 cubic inches

15. Elena's 6 quiz scores in her dental hygiene class were as follows:

84, 77, 98, 86, 95, 76

What is Elena's mean (average) score?

    (A) 77

    (B) 85

    (C) 86

    (D) 103.2

16. Mario is making pasta sauce for dinner. The family recipe includes the following ingredients:

- $\frac{3}{4}$ pound of ground beef
- 1 can of crushed tomatoes
- $\frac{1}{2}$ cup chopped onion
- $1\frac{1}{2}$ tsp dried basil

Mario decides to double the recipe because he is cooking for a big family gathering. Which of the following portions is the *incorrect* amount for the new proportions?

(A) 1.5 pounds ground beef

(B) 2 cans crushed tomatoes

(C) .25 chopped onions

(D) 3 tsps dried basil

17. Nedra has to walk from one location in a park to another spot. If she stays on paved paths, she will walk 2 blocks due south, then 3 blocks due east, and then another 2 blocks due south. If she had instead just walked a straight path from one spot to the other, how long a distance would that be? Assume that the blocks are squares.

(A) 3 blocks

(B) 4 blocks

(C) 5 blocks

(D) 7 blocks

18. In a standard deck of 52 playing cards, four of them are aces. If you draw eight cards from the deck and none of them are aces, what is the probability that the ninth card you draw is an ace?

(A) 1:44

(B) 1:13

(C) 1:11

(D) 1:9

Questions 19–20 refer to the following figure.

Object	Volume (in decibels)
Library	40
Electric Toothbrush	50
Freeway Traffic	70
Cicadas	80
Tractor	90
Snowmobile	100
Ambulance	120
Firecracker	150
Rifle	160

19. If your alarm clock goes off at 75 decibels, what fraction of the following items are louder than your alarm clock?

(A) 2/9

(B) 1/3

(C) 75/160

(D) 2/3

20. Cicadas are insects that appear every few years. They are known for their high-pitched singing. If cicadas were 50% more decibels than they currently are, they would be as loud as what object?

   (A) an ambulance

   (B) a rifle

   (C) a library

   (D) an electric toothbrush

21. Consider the equation for the volume of a sphere: $V = \frac{4}{3}\pi r^3$. If you have two spheres and one of them has a radius that is triple the radius of the other sphere, how much greater is the volume of that first sphere?

   (A) 3 times as large

   (B) 9 times as large

   (C) 12 times as large

   (D) 27 times as large

22. During their family reunion, 36 kids from the Johnson family go to the local water park to cool off. While there, they can go on the water slides, the lazy river, both, or neither. If 10 kids do both rides, 25 kids only do the lazy river, and 4 kids don't do either ride, how many kids ride just the water slides?

   (A) 7

   (B) 17

   (C) 21

   (D) 32

Answers and Explanations

In this section, I provide the answers and explanations to every question in the preceding practice tests. If you have the time, be sure to read the answer explanations. Doing so will help you understand why some answers were correct and others not, especially when the choices were really close. You can discover just as much from your errors as from the correct answers.

Reasoning through Language Arts answers

1. **C. willing to take a risk for a good return.** Choice (C) is correct because Carter left his job because of the lure of Arctic gold. The passage states that he's willing to take a risk for commensurate return. He isn't a romantic (Choice A) or a hardy native (Choice B), and he's certainly not a hero (Choice D).

2. **C. the drudgery of life as a clerk.** Carter wanted to escape his everyday drudgery in life as a clerk. "Bondage of commerce" refers to his dislike of his daily routine in the business world. Therefore, Choice (C) is correct. His need for returns, or wealth (Choice A), romance (Choice B), and risk-taking (Choice D) are different factors that don't apply to the question.

3. **B. to reach the Klondike.** According to the text, "Even its [the party's] goal . . . was the Klondike." Therefore, Choice (B) is correct, and the other choices are incorrect.

4. **D. ominous.** Choice (D) is correct because the chosen route to the Klondike seems ominous as there is a foreboding of ill-fortune throughout the passage. Words such as *unluckily*, *ominously*, and *evil star . . . in the ascendant* give the passage a feeling that something bad will happen. The route certainly wasn't blissful (Choice A) or scenic (Choice C), and *hardy* (Choice B) refers to a native of the region, so these choices are incorrect.

5. **D. He was a native of the Northwest.** The fact that Jacques was native-born and raised in the Northwest made him important to the party, so Choice (D) is correct. The facts that he was a renegade voyageur (Choice B), born of a Chippewa woman (Choice A) in a deerskin lodge (Choice C), though mentioned in the passage as true, aren't relevant to his importance to the party.

TIP

Did you select Choice A by mistake? Don't be fooled when all of the choices are mentioned in the passage. When this happens, it really pays to take time to read the question and all the answer choices. Only one of the choices will answer the question.

6. **A. their proposed route.** Choice (A) is stated directly in the second sentence of Paragraph 2. According to Paragraph 1, the search for gold motivated people to go to the Klondike, so Choices (B) and (C) are incorrect. Choice (D) is not described as unusual in the passage, and in any case, hiring a guide would be a likely course of action for a group of inexperienced travelers.

7. **C. to seek romance and adventure.** The passage says that Percy was seeking some romance and adventure in his otherwise mundane life. Choice (A) is mentioned in the passage to describe his personality but is not given as a reason for his joining the group. Choice (B) is incorrect because the passage says that he has an evil star, which means he suffers from bad luck, not that he himself is evil. Though the passage indicates that he is not wealthy, it does not say he seeks to get rich.

8. **C. He will die on the journey.** The passage says, "unluckily for his soul's welfare, he allied himself with a party of men." This statement implies that he will die on the trip. Words such as "ominously" and "evil star" also imply a bad ending to the adventure.

9. **A. has provided.** This choice is correct because the action started in the past and continues to the present. The clue is the phrase, "for over 80 years." For this reason, Choices (B) and (C) are incorrect. Choice (D) is not a complete verb, and so cannot be correct.

10. **A. Security or know.** Choice (A) is correct because Security must be capitalized because it's part of a proper noun, and no comma is needed to join two verbs with *and*. Therefore, Choices (B) and (C) are incorrect. *Knew* (Choice D) results in faulty parallel structure and does not make sense.

11. **B. survivors'.** Choice (B) is correct because *survivors* is plural. The possessive form of a plural noun ending in *-s* is formed by adding an apostrophe after the *-s: survivors'*. Therefore, the remaining choices are incorrect.

12. **B. customer service, and safeguarding.** Choice (B) is correct because commas are used to separate items in a list of three or more words or phrases joined by a word such as *and*. Choice (A) creates a sentence fragment followed by an awkward sentence. Choice (C) omits this comma and adds another, unnecessary comma. Choice (D) adds an unnecessary comma.

REMEMBER

Comma rules are not always clear-cut; some sources (but not the GED) omit the comma after the last item in a series. Luckily, this part of the comma rule is seldom tested, but the rules about other commas in a list or series are often on the test.

13. **B. retirement, we.** Choice (B) is correct because *retirement* results in correct parallel structure, and this choice includes the comma required after the introductory phrases. Choices (A) and (D) omit this comma. Choices (C) and (D) result in faulty parallel structure.

14. **A. account, we.** Choice (A) is correct because *whether* indicates the beginning of a dependent clause. When an independent clause comes after a dependent clause, a comma comes between the two clauses. Therefore, Choice (B) is incorrect. Choice (C) creates a sentence fragment. Choice (D) omits the subject of the independent clause and creates a dependent clause joined by a comma to a sentence fragment.

15. **A. this card.** Choice (A) is correct because, of the four choices, it's the clearest reference to "Cash Back Advantage credit card account." Choice (B) is vague. Choice (C) contains a double negative, *nobody*. Choice (D) is incorrect because "Cash Back Advantage credit card account" is singular and *them* is plural.

16. **C. will transition.** Choice (C) is correct because this sentence occurs with a number of other sentences in the future tense, so the future tense makes sense here. The other choices do not make sense.

17. **B. great features of your old.** Choice (B) is correct because the word *great* ("very good"), not its homonym *grate* ("metal screen"), is needed here, and *feature* should be plural. Therefore, the other choices are incorrect.

18. **D. every time.** Choice (D) is the only adverb that makes sense in the sentence. Choices (A) and (B) have faulty parallel structure. Choice (C) does not make sense.

19. **C. Previously,** Choice (C) is correct because the sentence is about the original credit card's benefits. Only Choice (C) indicates this relationship.

20. **B. You get that rate everywhere.** Choice (B) is the only choice that is a complete sentence and avoids a verb error. Choice (A) results in a sentence fragment. Choices (C) and (D) result in awkward and wordy sentences in the passive voice.

21. **A. on time using your card.** Only Choice (A) uses the phrases with the correct meaning. Choice (B) is confusing. Choice (C) is awkward and wordy. There is no reason to add *and*, so Choice (D) is incorrect.

22. **D. Your.** Choice (D) is correct because a possessive word is needed here. Therefore, the homonym *you're* (Choice B) is incorrect. Choice (A) is incorrect because a capital letter is needed at the beginning of every sentence. Choice (C) is possible, but Choice (D) is a more natural, usual sentence in written English.

23. **B. frequently.** Choice (B) is correct because an adverb is needed to modify an adjective such as *consumed*. The other choices are adjectives, so they are incorrect.

24. **D. But.** Choice (D), *But*, indicates the correct relationship between the ideas in the sentence and the one before it — contrast. The sentence does not propose an alternative, so Choice (A) is incorrect. The sentence does not add an idea, so Choices (B) and (C) are incorrect.

25. **B. contain.** Choice (B) is correct because the subject of the sentence is *ounces*, a plural noun. A plural verb, *contain*, is required to agree with its plural subject. If you selected Choice (A), you probably thought that *energy drink*, which is singular, was the subject. The noun that is closest to the verb is not always the subject. This question shows the value of reading all the choices before selecting your answer. Choices (C) and (D) are incorrect because there is no reason to use these past tense forms in this sentence.

26. **C. it's safe to consume up to 400 mg of caffeine per day.** Choice (C) uses the contraction *it's* correctly and avoids the errors in the other choices. Choice (A) creates a sentence fragment. Choice (B) is awkward and wordy. Choice (D) uses the possessive word *its* in place of *it's*.

27. **B. can affect.** Choice (B) is correct because it uses the verb *affect* correctly. Choices (A) and (C) use a homonym of *affect*, the noun *effect*, as a verb, and so are incorrect. Choice (D) uses the correct homonym but has an agreement error. The verb should be plural (*affect*) to agree with the plural subject *amounts*.

REMEMBER

A good way to remember the difference between the confusing homonyms *affect* and *effect* is that *affect* is a verb and *effect* is a noun.

28. **C. As.** Choice (C) is correct because this word best shows the relationship between the two parts of the sentences, which describes two things that happen at the same time. Choice (A) is incorrect because the sentence does not describe a cause–effect relationship. Choice (B) is incorrect because *during* is a preposition and so introduces a phrase not a clause. Choice (D) does not make sense.

29. **A. Dehydration coupled with increased heart rate and blood pressure.** Choice (A) is correct because only this choice has correct parallel structure. Choice (B) is incorrect because a word such as *elevated* is required before *blood pressure*. Choice (C) is missing such a word before *heart rate*. Choice (D) is missing this word entirely.

30. **A. energy, try.** Choice (A) is correct because a comma is needed to join a dependent clause to an independent clause. Therefore, Choice (B) is incorrect. Choices (C) and (D) create sentence fragments.

Extended Response sample

The following sample essay would receive solid marks. It isn't perfect, but as the GED Testing Service tells you, you're not expected to write the perfect essay. You're expected to write a good, first-draft-quality response. When you prepare your essay, consider using a schedule similar to this: 5 minutes to read and analyze the source passages, 10 minutes to prepare, 20 minutes to write, and the remaining 10 minutes to revise and edit.

Compare the following sample to the response you wrote and then compare your essay to the criteria the GED Testing Service uses to evaluate your writing:

>> Creation of an argument and use of evidence

>> Development and organizational structure

>> Clarity and command of standard English conventions

People continue to disagree as to whether video games are harmful or not. While there is evidence on both sides, the article, "Video Games Score High," presents the stronger argument.

The argument that video games cause violence is not convincing. The first article claims that there is a correlation between violence in the U.S. and increased game playing. However, the second article states that no reputable study has proven there is a link. In addition, people play these games in other countries where violence has not increased. So video games are probably not the cause of violence.

The first article says that video games encourage a sedentary lifestyle. It's true that people sit to play games, but most gamers I know take time for sports and exercise. People just need to manage their time playing.

Video games also seem to provide many benefits. People learn sportsmanship from games, as well as other valuable skills, such as teamwork. In addition, people have fun playing them. There is nothing like coming home from a long, frustrating day at work and playing a fun game with friends online. I often play a video game on study breaks while preparing for the GED. It helps me to relax so I can focus on learning.

For all these reasons, the second article makes a much stronger case. I will continue to play video games knowing that they are not harmful or bad.

Social Studies answers

1. **B. He wanted to show support for women's suffrage.** In several places throughout the passage, Twain mentions his support for extending voting rights to women, so Choice (B) is correct. He mentions corruption (Choice A) only with regard to women's votes ending it. Choice (C) is not mentioned in the passage. Though he speaks of his mother (Choice D), it's only to support his case that women deserve to vote.

2. **C. Women are better at stopping corruption than men.** While Twain was convinced that women should vote, the idea that women are better than men at stopping corruption is Twain's opinion (Choice C). The other choices are facts expressed in the excerpts.

3. **C. Women received the right to vote sooner that Twain predicted.** Choice (C) is correct because in the passage, Twain predicts it will take 25 years for women to get the right to vote. He spoke in 1901, and the amendment came into force in 1920, five to six years earlier than Twain predicted. Choice (A) is not supported by the passage. Choice (B) is contradicted by the amendment. The amendment states that the government will enforce this new right (Choice D).

4. **D. U.S involvement in the war was a failure.** Choice (D) is correct because the United States did not prevent Vietnam from becoming Communist. Therefore, Choices (B) and (C) are incorrect. The United States fought in Vietnam because they believed Choice (A) to be true, but it's not a conclusion that can be drawn from the information.

5. **C. a series of social media posts saying that the army is secretly getting ready to take over Washington, D.C.** Of all the choices, only Choice (C) is deliberately false or misleading, thus falling into the danger Madison warned of. The remaining choices are about topics that are routinely or recently reported on and are not false or misleading.

6. **B. President Trump issued more executive orders per year than the other three presidents in the table.** Choice (B) is correct because the table shows that President Trump issued 55 executive orders, which is more than the three previous presidents. Therefore, Choice (D) Is incorrect. There is not enough data about one-term presidents to support Choice (A). Choice (C) may be true but cannot be concluded from the table because it does not break out the orders by first or second term.

7. **B. Seema attends weekly prayers at her local mosque.** All the choices except Choice (B) are political rights, so this choice is correct.

8. **D. Voting patterns show that the United States is very divided politically.** Choice (D) is correct because the pattern shows that southern states as well as predominantly agricultural states are red, and more urban and industrial states are blue. In addition, only a few states are purple, which shows that most states are aligned with one party. While one hopes that Americans are interested in the future of the country (Choice A), this statement cannot be concluded from the map. Choice (B) is contradicted by the map. Some people may believe that Choice (C) is true, but it cannot be concluded from the map. In addition, in the U.S. system, there is no requirement that voters remain loyal to a party, though they have the right to do so.

9. **1B, 2B. enacts, judicial.** The role of the legislative branch is to pass, or enact (Item 1), new laws. The judicial branch (Item 2) interprets the laws and ensures that they are being applied properly.

10. **B. to add urgency to her message.** Information about the problems former tenants experience will encourage current tenants to take the matter seriously, so Choice (B) is correct. Choice (A) is not consistent with the purpose of the letter. The letter is directed to tenants, not management, so Choices (C) and (D) are incorrect.

11. **C. the right to petition for redress of grievances.** The association is a group of neighbors advocating for their rights, so the answer is Choice (C). Therefore, the other choices are incorrect.

12. **C. to prevent one part of government from becoming too powerful.** Choice (C) is correct because the system limits each branch's powers. Choice (A) is only partially correct, so it cannot be the answer. Choice (A) is a good example of why it's helpful to read all the answer choices before you select an answer; this can help you to avoid quickly selecting a choice that is only partially correct. Choices (B) and (D) are not relevant to the separation of powers.

Partially true answer choices are never correct! Always read all the answer choices to avoid selecting a partially true choice too hastily.

REMEMBER

13. **D. They are both limitations on the power of the federal government.** Choice (D) is correct because they define and limit the powers of the government. Choice (A) is incorrect because both of them are in the Constitution. Choice (B) is incorrect because freedom of religion is only in the Bill of Rights. Choice (C) is contradicted by the information.

14. **B. federalism.** The cartoon shows tension between the colonies acting together and keeping their freedom and autonomy. This is the same issue addressed by federalism, which clearly defines state and federal powers. Therefore, Choice (B) is correct. The remaining choices are not relevant to the cartoon.

15. **C. 2008.** The biggest increase was $0.80, which happened in 2008 (Choice C). The increase in 1997 was $0.40 (Choice A). The increase in 2007 was $0.70 (Choice B). The increase in 2009 was $0.60 (Choice D). As of the writing of this test, the minimum wage has not gone up.

Keep in mind that you can use the on-screen calculator or your own TI-30XS calculator (only when testing at a test center) for questions such as this one.

REMEMBER

16. **B. They were based on mortgages issued to people with poor credit.** Choice (B) is stated directly in the passage. The remaining choices by themselves are not enough to cause a problem.

17. **B. an online ad provider that controls most Internet advertising.** Choice (B) is the only choice that meets the definition of a monopoly — a company controlling an excessive part of a market or product. Choice (A) is incorrect because it is a utility and so is exempt from the laws against monopolies. Choice (C) is incorrect because even though that network is top-rated, there are many other networks available over the air and on cable. Choice (D) is incorrect because the laws don't apply to the toll road as it's not owned by a private company but by the public.

18. **A. Churchill respects Stalin as an ally but fears his present intentions.** It's clear from the information that though Churchill acknowledges Stalin as an ally, he distrusts Stalin's current actions in Europe, so Choice (A) is correct. For this reason, Choices (C) and (D) are incorrect. Choice (B) is contradicted by the information.

19. **B. Europe has been divided into one area with democratic governments and another under Communist dictatorships.** It's clear that Churchill believes that the new Communist governments are dictatorships, so Choice (B) is correct. Choice (A) confuses the literal with the figurative meaning of the phrase and so is incorrect. Choice (C) is incorrect because the countries remain intact; just their governments have changed. Choice (D) is contradicted by the information.

20. **D. Africa.** Of the top countries for refugees mentioned in the information, seven are in Africa. Therefore, Choice (D) is correct, and the other choices are incorrect.

Science answers

1. **B. brown.** According to the information, the parent with brown eyes has one copy of a blue allele and one copy of a brown allele. Therefore, brown (Choice B) is dominant.

2. **B. 2:4.** The Punnett square shows that 2 of the 4 possible genotypes for children from these parents have at least one copy of the allele for brown eyes. Therefore, Choice (B) is correct.

3. **D. Prevent people from going into piping plovers' nesting habitats.** Choice (D) is correct because this measure will ensure that nesting birds are not disturbed. Choice (A) will further reduce the population by reducing nesting sites. Choice (B) will result in an increase in predators, which will cause more reductions in the population. Choice (C) will likely increase traffic in nesting habitats and disturb the birds. Communities, however, do host information events away from the nesting sites, so people know to avoid the nesting areas. In 2019, a music festival in Chicago was cancelled because it was too near the nesting site of the first pair of piping plovers seen in Chicago for generations. Those birds got the rock star treatment!

4. **Flagella.** The long, tail-like structure is a flagella.

5. **A. Correlation does not show cause.** Choice (A) is correct because starting in 1795, the navy officials knew that consuming lemon juice prevented scurvy, but scientists did not know the cause was a lack of ascorbic acid until the 1930s. Choices (B) and (D) are contradicted by the information. Choice (C) cannot be concluded from the information, and most experts agree that taking such high doses is not necessary or advisable.

6. **C. the circulatory system.** The respiratory system and the circulatory (Choice C) system work together to bring oxygen to the body and remove carbon dioxide.

7. **D. independent — fertilizer; dependent — plant height.** Choice (D) is correct because the fertilizer is the variable that the researcher can control. The dependent variable is the result. Therefore, Choice (B) is incorrect. Choice (A) is incorrect because water and sunlight were not variables in this experiment. Choice (C) is incorrect because plant height, not water and sunlight, is the dependent variable.

REMEMBER

The dependent variable is called that because its change is dependent on the changes to the independent variable(s).

8. **C. Place both plants in places where light will not be blocked and switch the plants' positions once daily.** The problem in this situation is that the two plants got different amounts of sunlight in the late afternoon. Only Choice (C) will ensure that the position of the plants will not affect the average amount of sunlight they receive during the experiment. Choice (A) would help the plants grow straighter but would not ensure that they get equal amounts of sunlight. Choice (B) would give one of the plants an extra advantage over the other one and make the results unreliable. Choice (D) would likely decrease the light available to both plants but would still not ensure that they both get the same amount of sunlight.

9. **C. At the time, most of the medical community was not willing to pay attention to a woman.** Choice (C) is correct because at the time, most doctors were men, and people did not believe women made good doctors or scientists. Choice (A) is not supported by the information. People at the time knew that there were poisonous plants, but Bigsby couldn't figure out which one was responsible for milk sickness. Choice (B) is incorrect because Bigsby developed a hypothesis and tested it with the plant identified by the Shawnee woman. Choice (D) is contradicted by the information, which says that people respected her.

10. **A. The solubility of all four substances goes up as temperature increases.** The graph shows the solubility of all the substances increasing as the temperature rises, so Choice (A) is correct and Choice (C) is incorrect. The curves are different for each substance, so Choice (B) is incorrect. Choice (D) is not supported by the information in the graph. In fact, at 100° C, the water will start to boil, and as it converts to gas, the dissolved substances will precipitate.

11. **D. sodium chloride.** The curve for sodium chloride rises the least, so Choice (D) is correct.

12. **B. A child rolls a bowling ball, and it comes to a stop part-way down the alley.** Choice (B) is correct because friction and gravity caused the ball to stop midway along the alley. An adult bowler would likely throw the ball hard enough to overcome friction and gravity. Choice (A) is incorrect because another force was not applied to the ball — the player made a strike. Choice (C) is not possible because the vase is safe from having a force applied to it while locked in the cabinet. Choice (D) is incorrect because the meteor is continuing to travel in space, where there is no friction or headwind to slow it.

13. **A. inclined plane.** Choice (A) is correct because a ramp is an inclined plane. A ramp directs horizontal force upwards. Therefore, the other choices are incorrect.

14. **B. Without vitamin D, land vertebrates cannot absorb calcium needed for bone health.** Choice (B) is correct because this detail provides more information about the main benefit of UV to humans. Choices (A) and (C) are not relevant because they are about other kinds of light. Choice (D) adds a detail about light from the Sun, but it does not strengthen the main idea of the passage, which is about the benefits and harmful effects of UV light.

15. **D. Sound waves can travel through solid materials.** Choice (D) is correct because sound waves can travel through solid materials. In all likelihood, the sounds are traveling through a beam in the wall that extends up from the first floor and the nightclub. Choice (A) is not correct because the nightclub is in the front of the building and the apartment is in the back. Soundwaves cannot exit the nightclub through the front of the building and enter a window at the back of the building. Choice (B) is true but does not explain why Peter can hear music in his bedroom. Choice (C) is not possible because he would hear the music in the stairway, and the information says that he does not.

16. **B. The acidity of seawater will increase.** The effect of increased carbonic acid in the ocean is that the ocean's acidity will increase, so Choice (B) is correct and Choices (A) and (D) are incorrect. Choice (C) does not make sense because burning fossil fuel is the cause of increased carbon dioxide gas in the atmosphere.

17. **A. Governments need to take steps to manage high water levels in Lake Michigan.** Given the threat high water levels pose to so many people, Choice (A) is a logical conclusion. There is no evidence in the passage to support Choices (B) or (C). Choice (D) is contradicted by information in the passage.

18. **two.** The answer is two. The two independent variables are weather (dry or rainy) and temperature. If you thought that the answer was one (number of bats), then you mistook the dependent variable (number of bats) for an independent variable.

Math answers

1. **8.** To write in exponential notation, you move the decimal point to the left until there is only one number in front of it. Each move to the left represents one power of 10. So, for 354,000,000, you have to move it 8 spots to the left until you have just 3.54 in front. Because you move it 8 spots, that 8 is the value of the exponent, as it represents 8 powers of 10.

2. **C. 98.** To calculate this answer, start at number 8 and then add 15 each time to find the next person to receive a lottery ticket. Of the numbers in the choices, only 98 (Choice C) comes up.

   8, 23, 38, 53, 68, 83, **98**, 113

   TIP

   Unless you can add quickly in your head, using the calculator is the fastest and most accurate way to answer this question. Input 8 and keep adding 15 until you find one of the answer choices. Another way to reach the solution is to subtract 8 from each answer choice and then divide by 15. The first choice to be evenly divisible by 15 is the answer.

3. **D. 10.** To solve this problem, simply substitute the values for b and c, and solve using the correct order of operations, paying attention to signed (positive and negative) numbers.

   $(-3)^2 - (3 + 2 \times (-2)) = 9 - (3 - 4)$

   $= 9 - (-1) = 9 + 1 = 10$

   So, Choice (D) is correct. Choice (A) made two errors with negative numbers. The square of a negative number is always positive. In addition, 1 was subtracted instead of added. Choice (B) also forgot that the square of a negative number is always positive. Choice (C) added −1 instead of subtracting it.

4. C. 13 3-oz. jars and 36 6-oz. jars. To answer this question, you need to calculate the amount of jam each combination of jars will hold. Choice (A) will hold more than 255 ounces, so it is incorrect: $15 \times 3 + 18 \times 12 = 45 + 216 = 261$ ounces.

Choice (B) will also hold more than 255 ounces: $7 \times 6 + 9 \times 24 = 42 + 216 = 258$.

Choice (C) results in exactly 255 ounces so is correct:

$13 \times 3 + 36 \times 6 = 39 + 216 = 255$ ounces.

Because only one choice is correct, you can simply double-check your calculation for Choice (C) and skip Choice (D), which will also hold more than 255 ounces: $13 \times 18 + 4 \times 24 = 234 + 96 = 330$.

TIP

On a question like this one, it's important to pay attention to order of operations. Remember to multiply from left to right and then add from left to right. Because you have to calculate the contents of each combination of jars, this question also will take a long time to answer. Therefore, it's one you might skip until later in the test.

5. $3.57. 3 dozen donuts would cost $3 \times \$9.49 = \$28.47$.

36 individual donuts would cost $36 \times \$0.89 = \$32.04$.

Therefore, the amount you would save would be $\$32.04 - \$28.47 = \$3.57$.

6. C. 6%. To find the tax rate, take the difference between the price paid ($21.20) and the price listed ($20): $\$21.20 - \$20 = \$1.20$. Take that result and divide it by the original price ($20). That percentage is the tax rate: $1.20 / 20 = 0.06 = 6\%$. So, Choice (C) is correct.

7. A. 1 hour, 15 minutes. If the normal commute takes half an hour at 40 mph, that means the commute is $0.5 \times 40 = 20$ miles. Thus, 20 miles at 16 mph = $20 \div 16 = 1.25$ hours, which is 1 hour and 15 minutes. (A quarter of an hour is 15 minutes.) Choice (B) is incorrect because it confuses .25 hours with 25 minutes. Choice (C) does not make sense. Choice (D) forgot to calculate the distance of Caleb's commute (20 miles) and used his driving speed (40 mph) instead: $40/16 = 2.5$.

8. C. –4/5. The slope of a line is equal to the change in the *y* coordinates divided by the change in the *x* coordinates. In this case, from intercept to intercept, the *y* coordinates went down 4, while the *x* coordinates went up 5, making the slope equal to $-4/5$.

9. D. a 14-inch pineapple and ham pizza with a medium drink. A good way to approach questions like this one is to look for choices that are likely to be too expensive and try those first. Start with the option that has the most expensive pizza selection: the rectangular cheese pizza with small drink (Choice A) costs $\$17.99 + \$2 = \$19.99$. John can afford that one, so Choice (A) is not the answer. The next order most likely to be too expensive is Choice (D), a 14-inch pineapple and ham pizza with a medium drink. That order costs $\$15.99 + \$2 + \$2.50 = \$20.49$. That's more than $20, so Choice (D) is the answer. Plus, it has pineapple and ham on it, which is just wrong!

WARNING

Be careful with questions that use negative words such as *not*. Sometimes you may read too quickly and skip over the negative word in the question, Then, it's easy to select the first answer choice as correct. These kinds of questions show the value of reading the question carefully. This kind of question is not that common but can come up occasionally. When they do, the test makers usually, but not always, put the negative word in capital letters and/or boldface type.

10. **D. $660.** Choice (D) is correct because if he works 50 hours in one week, he gets paid $12 per hour for the first 40 hours and then he gets an additional 50% pay for the last 10 hours.

$12 × 40 = $480

$12 × 10 + $12 × 10 × .5 = $120 + $60 = $180

$480 + $180 = $660

Choice (A) is the pay he will receive for the 10 hours over 40 hours. Choice (B) is his regular pay for working 40 hours in a week. Choice (C) is his pay for working 50 hours in a week without the extra pay for working more than 40 hours.

REMEMBER

Like question 4, this question requires correct order of operation: Multiply from left to right and then add from left to right. If you use your calculator correctly, it will automatically use correct order of operation, which can be a big time saver. Just remember to input the whole expression. Try it now, and see for yourself!

11. **B. 96.** One way to find the least common multiple of two numbers is to just start listing the multiples of each number until you get one that is common to both.

Multiples of 24: 24, 48, 72, **96**, 120

Multiples of 32: 32, 64, **96**, 128

The first multiple that is common to both is 96 (Choice B). Choice (A) is a common factor to both, not a common multiple. Choice (C) is a multiple of only 32. Choice (D) is a common multiple of both but is not the least common multiple.

TIP

You can easily eliminate Choice (A) as incorrect because it is smaller than both 24 and 32, so cannot be a multiple of the numbers. This can help you if you run out of time and have to guess. Eliminating even one of the choices improves your odds of guessing correctly.

12. **C. 10.5.** According to the graph, people in the 25–34 age group average 3.5 hours of daily Internet usage. Therefore, over a 3-day weekend, you would expect a 30-year-old to average 3 × 3.5 = 10.5 hours (Choice C).

Choice (A) shows average usage for this age group over a two-day weekend. Choice (B) shows average usage for a 3-day weekend for a 35- to 44-year-old. Choice (D) shows average usage for a 16- to 24-year-old over the same time period.

13. **C. 35–44 and 45–54.** Choice (C) is correct because the difference between the 35–44 and 45–54 age groups is one hour of average daily Internet usage: 3 – 2 = 1.

Every other pairing of age groups has a difference of 0.5 hour.

14. **A. 257.5 cubic inches.** The answer is Choice (A). To figure it out, use the formulas in the formula sheet to calculate the volume of the prism and the volume of the cylinder. Then subtract. Keep in mind that the radius of the circle (5 inches) means that each side of the base of the square prism measures 10 inches.

The volume of a prism is $V = l \times w \times h = 10 \times 10 \times 12 = 1,200$.

The volume of a cylinder is $V = \pi r^2 \times h = 5^2 \times 12 \times \pi = 942.47$, which rounds to 942.5.

So, the difference between the prism and the cylinder is 1,200 – 942.5 = 257.5 (Choice A).

Choice (B) is the volume of the cylinder. Choice (C) is the volume of the prism. Choice (D) is the sum of the two volumes, not the difference.

TIP

If you don't know the meaning of the word *inscribed*, you can use the diagram to help you. It shows that the cylinder is inside the square prism. Diagrams can often help you figure out the meaning of unfamiliar words.

15. **C. 86.** The mean of the six scores is $\frac{84+77+98+86+95+76}{6} = \frac{516}{6} = 86$

Therefore, Choice (C) is correct.

16. **C. .25 chopped onions.** Remember, on this item, you are looking for the answer choice that is incorrect. To figure out the answer, multiply all the ingredients by 2. To save time, compare each result to its answer choice. When you find the choice that is incorrect, you have found the answer.

$2 \times \frac{3}{4} = 1.5$ pounds ground beef (Choice A)

$2 \times 1 = 2$ cans crushed tomatoes (Choice B)

$2 \times \frac{1}{2} = 1$ cup chopped onions (Choice C)

Choice (C) incorrectly divides by 2 instead of multiplying, so it is the answer. You can stop calculating at this point and go on to the next item. For reference, here is the calculation for Choice (D): $2 \times 1\frac{1}{2} = 2 \times \frac{3}{2} = 3$ tsp dried basil.

17. **C. 5 blocks.** To help you answer this question, make a drawing of the path Nedra follows.

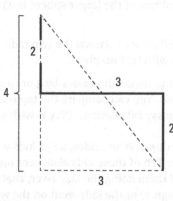

If Nedra were to walk directly from the starting point to the finishing point in a straight line, that would be equivalent to the hypotenuse of a right triangle with sides 3 and 4 (see diagram). Using the Pythagorean Theorem, which is on the formula sheet, the length of the hypotenuse would be

$3^2 + 4^2 = x^2$

$9 + 16 = x^2$

$25 = x^2$

$5 = x$

So, Choice (C) is correct. Choices (A) and (B) are the base and height of the triangle. Choice (D) is the number of blocks actually walked $(2 + 3 + 2 = 7)$, not the length of the hypotenuse.

Using the erasable tablet or online whiteboard to make a diagram can help you with questions like this one.

TIP

18. **C. 1:11.** The chance of drawing an ace from a standard deck of playing cards is 4:52. If you remove 8 cards and none of them are aces, then the chance now becomes 4:44. That simplifies to 1:11 (Choice C). Choice (A) is the odds of drawing a certain ace, say the ace of hearts. Choice (B) is the odds of drawing one of the aces before 8 cards are removed. Choice (D) does not make sense.

19. **D. 2/3.** Of the 9 objects in the list, 6 have decibel levels higher than 75, so the fraction of items louder than 75 is 6/9, which simplifies to 2/3.

20. **A. an ambulance.** According to the table, cicadas have a decibel level of 80. $50\% \times 80 = 40$. So if cicadas were 50% higher decibel level, their decibel level would be $80 + 40 = 120$, which is the decibel level of an ambulance.

21. **D. 27 times as large.** Try this with actual numbers. If the original radius is 2, then the volume of the sphere is $V = \frac{4}{3}\pi 2^3 = \frac{4}{3}\pi \times 8 = \frac{32}{3}\pi$.

    Now triple the radius so that it equals 6.

    Now the volume of the sphere is $V = \frac{4}{3}\pi 6^3 = \frac{4}{3}\pi \times 216 = \frac{864}{3}\pi$.

    And because $864 \div 32 = 27$, that means the volume of the larger sphere is 27 times as large as the original sphere (Choice D).

    If you selected Choice (A), you selected the difference between the two radii. Remember that it's always a good idea to test a formula with real numbers.

    TIP

    Note the nifty math shortcut: You don't need to divide the values by 3 or multiply by pi, because these operations are in both equations. You can compare the top numbers in the fractions directly. That helps avoid a lot of messy calculations. (Try it with your calculator.)

22. **A. 7.** The total is 36 kids in all. Four kids didn't go on any rides, so 32 kids went on rides. You know that 25 kids went on the lazy river. Ten of those kids also went on the water slides. With 32 kids going on rides, and 25 of them doing the lazy river, that leaves 7 who did just the water slides ($32 - 25 = 7$). Although 17 of the kids went on the water slides, 10 of them also went on the lazy river. So, the answer is Choice (A). Choice (B) is the total number of kids who went on the water slides. Choice (C) doesn't exclude the kids who didn't go on any rides. Choice (D) is the total number of kids who went on rides.

Block 5

Ten Tips for the Night Before Your Test

Of course, you want to do well on the GED — otherwise, you wouldn't be reading this book. But you also know that your time is limited, so this chapter gives you ten ideas and tips for the night before the test. These tips are all part of preparing for the big day. You want to be able to arrive at the test site with the least amount of worry and stress. Removing as many sources of stress as possible before that day will make everything go more smoothly.

Know Your Time-Management Strategies

The GED is a timed test, so having a time-management strategy will help you do well. Here's a review of the key tips:

>> Because you know how many questions you'll have to answer and how much time you have to answer each one, you can do some quick math to determine how much time you have to answer each question.

>> Use the on-screen timer to make sure you stay on track to finish the test on time.

>> While you're taking the Extended Response section of the language arts test, you can block your time using the suggestions in Block 2.

>> If you're struggling with a question, use the Flag for Review button so you can return to the question after you've answered the questions you're more confident about.

Review Strategies for Analyzing and Answering Questions

As I explain in Block 1, having a few GED test-taking strategies will help you do well on the test. Obviously, the most important way to prepare for the GED is to read a lot, take practice tests, and find help with concepts you don't understand yet. However, the following test-taking tips can also help you gain a few points that just might get to you to your desired score:

>> Identify what the question is asking. If you clearly understand the question, you're more likely to choose the correct answer.

>> Eliminate obviously wrong answers.

>> Guess the answer from among the likely questions if you don't know. You don't lose points for wrong answers on the GED.

See Block 1 for more details about these strategies.

Take a Practice Test

Taking practice tests before you take the actual test will help you get familiar with the test format, the types of questions you'll be asked, and what subject areas you may need to work on. Take as many practice tests as you can before test day, starting with the practice test that comes with this book. Be sure to practice with the time limits, too.

If you have time for more practice than this book offers, the GED Testing Service also provides some free practice tests at www.gedtestingservice.com/educators/freepracticetest.

Practice Your Stress-Coping Strategies

Do tests make you anxious? You're not alone. It's normal to feel stressed while you're taking a test, and you can get through that stress more easily if you practice your coping strategies before you're in the testing room. If you need tips or ideas for coping with stress during the test, see Block 1.

Set Up Your Test Area or Plan Your Route to the Test Site

On certain days and occasions, you just don't want to be late, get lost, or have a problem. These days include your wedding day, the day of an important job interview, and the day you're taking the GED. So, be prepared, whether you're taking the test at home or at a test center.

If you're taking the test at home, both your computer and the room you test in have to meet special requirements. Don't leave this to the last minute. Check the latest requirements on the GED website (https://ged.com) and the email you receive when you sign up for the test. The night before the test, double-check that you can meet all the requirements. You can view these requirements at https://ged.com/take-the-ged-test-online.

TIP

If you take the GED at home, you need to work in a private room with no interruptions. If you have roommates, make arrangements well before test day. If you have children, ask another person to keep an eye on them during the test so you can concentrate!

TIP

No matter where you test — at home or at a testing center — arrange your work area. Make sure that your chair is at a comfortable height, arrange the keyboard and mouse, and adjust the height and angle of the screen. If you're left-handed, you may need to move the mouse to the left of the keyboard. Make sure you allow time to do this before your test starts! If you test at home, the only drink you're allowed to have is water in a clear container. So get a clear water bottle ready if you think you'll get thirsty. Just save your fancy colored goblets for the victory celebration after you pass the test!

If you're going to a testing center to take the test, make sure you're prepared. Plan a route to the testing site from your home or job or wherever you'll be commuting from. Map it out and practice getting to the test center. If you're driving to the test center, make sure you know where to park. Arrive early enough so you can be sure to find a spot. *Remember:* You can't leave your car in the middle of the street if you expect to drive it home, too!

TIP

Leave extra time for surprises. You never know when your street could be declared the site for an elephant crossing or be closed for construction. The crowd, elephants, or construction zone detours could make you late for the test unless you allow yourself some extra time.

Lay Out Comfortable Clothes

When you're taking the GED, you don't want to worry about being so cold or hot that you can't focus. Choose comfortable clothes and plan to dress in layers, so you can focus on the test instead of what you're wearing.

Have Your Picture ID Ready

To take the GED, you need an acceptable picture ID. Because what's *acceptable* may vary from state to state, check with your state GED office or your local testing center (or check the information that they send you after you register) before the test.

REMEMBER

The picture ID required is usually a driver's license, state ID card, passport, or other government-issued ID (including a *matricula consular* issued by a Mexican consulate in the United States). At any rate, it's usually something common and easy to get — *if you plan ahead!* Just check in advance for what's required and make sure that you have it ready and with you on test day.

Work with the Computer, Calculator, and Formula Sheet

On the real GED, you'll be typing on a keyboard, using a mouse to select or drag items, and reading and digesting information on the screen. You'll also be using an on-screen or real scientific calculator. If you're new to any of these features of the computerized test and you have access to a computer at home, practice using them for a short time the night before.

Make sure that you're familiar with the layout of the screens on the test. Luckily, the screen layout is the same whether you test at home or at a testing center. (Check out Chapter 2 for information on the screen layout of each test.) Then use the free test at https://ged.com/study/free_online_ged_test. Finally, the GED Ready Practice Test will let you know for sure whether you have the computer skills you need to succeed.

Get familiar with the TI-30XS MultiView calculator, too — the handheld or on-screen version, whichever you'll be using. It's a scientific calculator with a lot of functions, not all of which you'll use on the test. The GED Testing Service's website (https://ged.com), has a number of calculator resources, including a reference sheet that shows you all the features you need to know, a tutorial that walks you through using the calculator, and an actual on-screen calculator emulator you can practice with.

Whether you bring your own TI-30XS MultiView calculator or use the on-screen version (a requirement if you test at home), prepare with the calculator you'll actually use. You don't want to be fumbling on test day.

The Math section has a formula sheet that can help you a lot. As you get familiar with the computer, find out the location of the formula sheet. You can reference the formula sheet at any time during the test, which can help you avoid depending on your memory on test day. Nevertheless, you may want to memorize a few easy and commonly used formulas, too, such as the area of a rectangle.

Visualize Success!

To make yourself less anxious about the GED, visualize yourself taking the test on test day. In your mind, see yourself entering the room, sitting down at the computer, and reaching out to the keyboard. Go through this routine in your mind until it begins to feel familiar. Then see yourself starting the test and scrolling through the questions (questions that are likely familiar to you because you've taken at least one practice test). See yourself noting the easy questions and beginning to answer them. By repeating this visual sequence over and over again in your mind, it becomes familiar — and what's familiar isn't nearly as stressful as what's unfamiliar. (This process, by the way, is called *visualization*, and it really works to put your mind at ease for the test.) And if you're taking the test at home, you can set up your test area and practice this routine for real!

Getting Good Rest the Week Before the Test

As part of your plan for preparation, include some social time, some downtime, and plenty of rest time because everyone performs better when well rested. In fact, your memory and ability to solve problems improve markedly when you're properly rested.

REMEMBER

Whatever you do, don't panic about your upcoming test and stay up all night (or every night for a week) right before the test. Instead, plan your week so you get plenty of sleep and are mentally and physically prepared for the test.

Index

A

accommodations, asking for, 5
active reading, 23
agreement, proper, 28
algebra, basic, 40
American history, as content for Social Studies test, 11
analysis questions, 22
answers. *see* practice questions and answers
artwork, 32–33
axes, on graphs, 37

B

bar graphs, 37
Bloch, Robert (author), 46

C

calculator, 6, 9, 40–41, 153–154
capitalization, 27
captions, on photos, 38
Churchill, Winston (Prime Minister), 123–124
CIA Feature Story, 65
circle graphs, 37
civics and government, as content for Social Studies test, 11
clicking and dragging, with mouse, 8–9
clothing, 6, 153
column graphs, 37
comma splice, 56
command of evidence questions, 22
community materials, as source texts, 11
compass, on maps, 38
complex sentences, 28
compound sentence, 56
comprehension questions, 22

D

data analysis, 40
Declaration of Independence, 62–63
Department of Agriculture, 78
diagrams, interpreting, 37
dictionaries, 23
disability accommodations, asking for, 5
drag-and-drop questions, 13–14
drop-down menu questions, 14, 15

computers, 7–9, 153–154
contractions, 28
coordinate plane, 40

E

earth science, 12, 35
economics, as content for Social Studies test, 11
editing essays, 25–26
eligibility, for GED, 4
energy and related systems, 35
English keyboard, 8
essays
  planning, 24–25 (*see also* Reasoning through Language Arts (RLA) Extended Response)
  time for, 10
essential clause, 57
exam room rules, 7

F

fill-in-the-blank questions, 9, 14, 15
Flag for Review button, 16, 18
format, of Science test, 34–35
formula sheets, 40–41, 153–154
Franklin, Benjamin, 122
functions, in Mathematical Reasoning test, 40

G

GED
  about, 3
  preparing for, 21–41
  registering for, 4–6
  retaking, 19
  what to bring, 6
  what to expect, 7–15
GED Testing Service (website), 6, 9
geography and the world, as content for Social Studies test, 12
geometry, 40
Glenn Research Center (website), 73, 78
Grammar and Language section
  about, 27–29
  sample questions and answers, 51–58
  time for, 10
graphs
  about, 30–31
  interpreting, 37
  in Mathematical Reasoning test, 40

H

homonyms, 56
human health and living systems, 35

I

icons, explained, 2
ID, 6, 153
"In a Far Country" (London), 105
incomplete sentences, 28
informational works, as source texts, 11
intelligent guessing, 17–18

J

Jackson, William A., 65

K

keyboards, typing on, 8
Khan Academy, 39

L

labels
  on graphs and diagrams, 37
  on maps, 38
  on photos, 38
language options, 5
legends
  on graphs, 37
  on maps, 38
life science, 12, 35
line graphs, 37
literature, as source texts, 11
location, for GED, 4
London, Jack (author), 105
"A Look Back . . . The Black Dispatches: Intelligence During the Civil War," 65

M

Madison, James, 64
maps, 30, 31, 38
Mathematical Reasoning test
  about, 13, 39
  calculators, 40–41
  formula sheets, 40–41
  math skills needed for, 39–40
  practice test, 131–138, 146–150
  sample questions and answers, 91–101
  special symbols, 40–41
  time for, 10
measurement, 40
mechanics, in Grammar and Language section, 27–28
mouse, clicking and dragging with, 8–9
multiple-choice questions, 13, 14

N

NASA, 73, 76, 77, 78, 80, 84–85
non-essential clause, 57
number operations, 39
number sense, 39

O

Occupational Safety & Health Administration, 80–81, 85

Office of Response and Restoration, 81

online resources, for science material, 34

on-screen calculator, 9

on-screen whiteboard, 9

P

photographs, 32–33, 38

physical science, 12, 34–35

picture ID, 6, 153

pie graphs/charts, 37

political cartoons, 32

possessives, 28

practice questions and answers

  about, 43

  Mathematical Reasoning test, 91–101

  RLA Extended Response, 49–51

  RLA Grammar and Language, 51–58

  RLA Reading Comprehension, 43–49

  Science test, 73–90

  Social Studies test, 58–72

practice tests

  about, 103

  importance of taking, 152

  Mathematical Reasoning, 131–138, 146–150

  Reasoning through Language Arts, 103–111, 138–141

  Reasoning through Language Arts Extended Response, 112–115, 141–142

  Science, 125–131, 144–146

  Social Studies, 116–124, 142–144

prompt, reading and annotating, 24

punctuation, 28

Q

questions

  about text passages, 29–30

  about visual materials, 30–33

  addressing and answering, 17

  analysis, 22

  fill-in-the-blank, 9, 14, 15

  multiple-choice, 13, 14

  reading comprehension, 22

  solving with/without calculators, 41

  tips for analyzing and answering, 152

  types of, 13–15

R

reading, developing skills for, 22–23

reading glasses, 6

reading speed, 23

Reading through Comprehension section

  sample questions and answers, 43–49

  time for, 10

Reasoning through Language Arts (RLA) Extended Response

  about, 23–24

  checking for winning essays, 26

  editing and revising, 25–26

  improving essay writing skills, 26–27

  planning essay, 24–25

  practice test, 112–115, 141–142

  reading and annotating prompt, 24

  sample questions and answers, 49–51

  time for, 10

  writing, 25

Reasoning through Language Arts (RLA) test

  about, 10–11, 21

  Grammar and Language section, 27–29

  practice test, 103–111, 138–141

  Reading Comprehension section, 21–23

  Reading through Comprehension Extended Response section, 23–27

  time for, 10

registering, for GED, 4–6

Remember icon, 2

rest, importance of, 154

retaking GED, 19

revising essays, 25–26

run-on sentence, 56

S

scale, on maps, 38
Science test
  about, 12, 33
  analyzing scientific text passages, 35–36
  format and topics for, 34–35
  interpreting graphs, tables, and visual materials, 36–38
  online practice for, 34
  practice test, 125–131, 144–146
  sample questions and answers, 73–90
  time for, 10
scientific text passages, analyzing, 35–36
scoring, 19
sentence fragment, 57
shoes, 6
signing up, for GED, 6
skills
  improving for essay-writing, 26–27
  needed for Mathematical Reasoning test, 39–40
Smith, Adam (economist), 68
Smithsonian National Museum of American History, 33
Social Studies test
  about, 11–12, 29
  practice test, 116–124, 142–144
  questions about text passages, 29–30
  questions about visual materials, 30–33
  sample questions and answers, 58–72
  time for, 10
source texts, 11
space science, 12, 35
special symbols, 40–41
spelling, 28
strategies, for test-taking, 15–18
stress management, 16, 152
success, visualizing, 154
synthesis questions, 22

T

tables, 31–32, 36
tablet whiteboard, 9
test area, setting up, 152–153
test site, planning route to, 152–153
test-taking strategies, 15–18
text passages, questions about, 29–30
"This Crowded Earth" (Bloch), 46
time
  for GED, 4, 10
  leaving for review, 18
  management strategies for, 151
  tips for, 16–17
Tip icon, 2
titles
  on graphs and diagrams, 37
  on maps, 38
topics, on Science test, 34–35
Tubman, Harriet, 65
Twain, Mark, 117
typing, on keyboards, 8

U

United States Geological Service Newsroom, 44
U.S. Department of Energy, 80
U.S. Environmental Protection Agency, 73, 75, 79, 81, 82, 83
U.S. founding documents, as source texts, 11
U.S. History For Dummies (Wiegand), 59, 60, 63, 66, 67–68
U.S. Surgeon General, 75
usage, 28–29

V

visual materials
  about, 36
  diagrams, 37
  graphs, 30–31, 37, 40

maps, 30, 31, 38
photographs, 32–33, 38
questions about, 30–33
tables, 31–32, 36
Votes for Women speech (Twain), 117

W

Warning icon, 2
The Wealth of Nations (Smith), 68
websites
  CIA Feature Story, 65
  Department of Agriculture, 78
  GED Testing Service, 6, 9
  Glenn Research Center, 73, 78
  Khan Academy, 39
  NASA, 73, 76, 77, 78, 80, 84–85

Occupational Safety & Health Administration, 80–81, 85
Office of Response and Restoration, 81
Smithsonian National Museum of American History, 33
United States Geological Service Newsroom, 44
U.S. Department of Energy, 80
U.S. Environmental Protection Agency, 73, 75, 79, 81, 82, 83
U.S. Surgeon General, 75
whiteboard, 9
Wiegand, Steve (author), 59, 60, 63, 66, 67–68
Womenshealth.gov, 74
word order, 28
workplace materials, as source texts, 11
writing essays, 25

maps, 30, 31, 38
photographs, 32–33, 38
questions about, 30–33
scales, 81, 32, 36
Votes for Women speech (Twain), 117

W

Warning icons, 2
The Wealth of Nations (Smith), 68
websites
CIA Feature Story, 65
Department of Agriculture, 74
SRP Testing Service, 6, 8,
Glenn Research Center, 73, 75
Khan Academy, 39
NASA, 73, 76, 77, 78, 80, 84–85,

Occupational Safety & Health Administration, 80–81, 83
Office of Response and Restoration, 81
Smithsonian National Museum of American History, 23
United States Geological Service, newsroom, 44
U.S. Department of Energy, 20
U.S. Environmental Protection Agency, 73–75, 79, 81, 82, 83
U.S. Surgeon General, 75
whiteboard, 9
Wiegand, Steve (author), 59, 60, 63, 66, 67–68
Womenshistory.gov, 24
word order, 28
workplace materials, as source texts, 14
writing essay, 25

About the Authors

For more than 25 years, Tim Collins, PhD, has specialized in materials development for the GED, and his books and media publications have helped countless learners pass this life-changing test.

Altogether, he has worked in the field of education for more than 40 years, and he has taught learners of all ages and backgrounds from early childhood to adult. He began his career as a high school teacher in Morocco, where, as part of a school-wide improvement program, he helped his school reduce the number of dropouts while aiding school-leavers to pass the required graduation test. As a result of this community-wide effort, the graduation rate increased from one of the lowest in the country to one of the highest. Since then, he has taught young children in Spain; university students in China, Spain, and the United States; and adult learners in the United States. Beginning in 1987, he began to specialize in materials development and worked for several major publishers.

Tim knows the challenges of pursuing education as an adult. While working full time, he completed his PhD at the University of Texas at Austin. After that, he worked as a professor at a major U.S. college of education for 15 years, where he helped prepare teachers to meet the challenges of today's elementary, middle school, and high school classrooms. Tim currently manages international education programs while continuing to develop materials that give adult learners the skills they need to succeed.

Publisher's Acknowledgments

Executive Editor: Lindsay Lefevere

Compiling Editor: Rebecca Huehls

Editor: Elizabeth Kuball

Production Editor: Pradesh Kumar

Cover Design: Wiley

Cover Image: © bortonia/Getty Images

Leverage the power

Dummies is the global leader in the reference category and one of the most trusted and highly regarded brands in the world. No longer just focused on books, customers now have access to the dummies content they need in the format they want. Together we'll craft a solution that engages your customers, stands out from the competition, and helps you meet your goals.

Advertising & Sponsorships

Connect with an engaged audience on a powerful multimedia site, and position your message alongside expert how-to content. Dummies.com is a one-stop shop for free, online information and know-how curated by a team of experts.

- Targeted ads
- Video
- Email Marketing

- Microsites
- Sweepstakes sponsorship

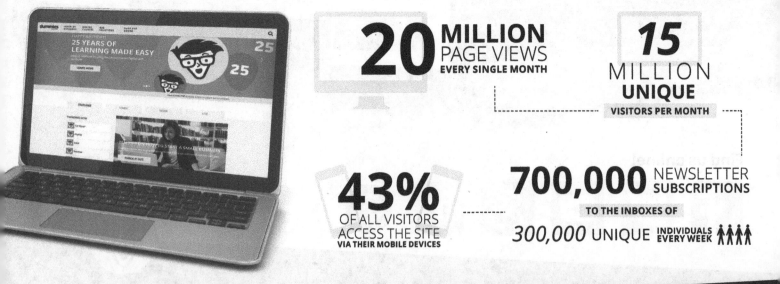

20 MILLION PAGE VIEWS EVERY SINGLE MONTH

15 MILLION UNIQUE VISITORS PER MONTH

43% OF ALL VISITORS ACCESS THE SITE VIA THEIR MOBILE DEVICES

700,000 NEWSLETTER SUBSCRIPTIONS TO THE INBOXES OF *300,000* UNIQUE INDIVIDUALS EVERY WEEK

# of dummies

Custom Publishing

Reach a global audience in any language by creating a solution that will differentiate you from competitors, amplify your message, and encourage customers to make a buying decision.

- Apps
- Books
- eBooks
- Video
- Audio
- Webinars

Brand Licensing & Content

Leverage the strength of the world's most popular reference brand to reach new audiences and channels of distribution.

For more information, visit **dummies.com/biz**

PERSONAL ENRICHMENT

Staying Sharp dummies
9781119187790
USA $26.00
CAN $31.99
UK £19.99

Facebook dummies
Carolyn Abram
9781119179030
USA $21.99
CAN $25.99
UK £16.99

Guitar dummies
9781119293354
USA $24.99
CAN $29.99
UK £17.99

Investing dummies
Eric Tyson, MBA
9781119293347
USA $22.99
CAN $27.99
UK £16.99

Beekeeping dummies
Howland Blackiston
9781119310068
USA $22.99
CAN $27.99
UK £16.99

Digital Photography dummies
Julie Adair King
9781119235606
USA $24.99
CAN $29.99
UK £17.99

Meditation dummies
Stephan Bodian
9781119251163
USA $24.99
CAN $29.99
UK £17.99

Pregnancy ALL-IN-ONE dummies 6 Books
9781119235491
USA $26.99
CAN $31.99
UK £19.99

Samsung Galaxy S7 dummies
Bill Hughes
9781119279952
USA $24.99
CAN $29.99
UK £17.99

iPhone dummies
Edward C. Baig
Bob "Dr. Mac" LeVitus
9781119283133
USA $24.99
CAN $29.99
UK £17.99

Crocheting dummies
Karen Manthey
Susan Brittain
9781119287117
USA $24.99
CAN $29.99
UK £16.99

Nutrition dummies
Carol Ann Rinzler
9781119130246
USA $22.99
CAN $27.99
UK £16.99

PROFESSIONAL DEVELOPMENT

Windows 10 dummies
Andy Rathbone
9781119311041
USA $24.99
CAN $29.99
UK £17.99

AutoCAD dummies
Bill Fane
9781119255796
USA $39.99
CAN $47.99
UK £27.99

Excel 2016 dummies
Greg Harvey, PhD
9781119293439
USA $26.99
CAN $31.99
UK £19.99

QuickBooks 2017 dummies
Stephen L. Nelson, MBA, CPA, MS in Taxation
9781119281467
USA $26.99
CAN $31.99
UK £19.99

macOS Sierra dummies
Bob "Dr. Mac" LeVitus
9781119280651
USA $29.99
CAN $35.99
UK £21.99

LinkedIn dummies
Joel Elad, MBAs
9781119251132
USA $24.99
CAN $29.99
UK £17.99

Windows 10 ALL-IN-ONE dummies 10 Books
Woody Leonhard
9781119310563
USA $34.00
CAN $41.99
UK £24.99

SharePoint 2016 dummies
Rosemarie Withee
Ken Withee
9781119181705
USA $29.99
CAN $35.99
UK £21.99

Fundamental Analysis dummies
Matt Krantz
9781119263593
USA $26.99
CAN $31.99
UK £19.99

Networking dummies
Doug Lowe
9781119257769
USA $29.99
CAN $35.99
UK £21.99

Office 2016 dummies
Wallace Wang
9781119293477
USA $26.99
CAN $31.99
UK £19.99

Office 365 dummies
Rosemarie Withee
Ken Withee
Jennifer Reed
9781119265313
USA $24.99
CAN $29.99
UK £17.99

Salesforce.com dummies
Liz Kao
Jon Paz
9781119239314
USA $29.99
CAN $35.99
UK £21.99

Coding dummies
Nikhil Abraham
9781119293323
USA $29.99
CAN $35.99
UK £21.99

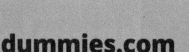
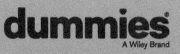

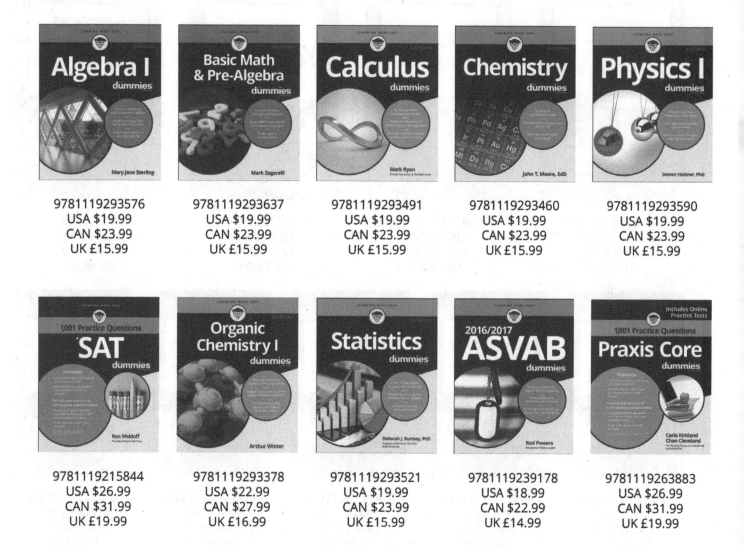

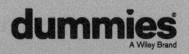